SURVIVAL ON THE DEATH RAILWAY AND NAGASAKI

JIM BRIGGINSHAW

SURVIVAL ON THE DEATH RAILWAY AND NAGASAKI

JIM BRIGGINSHAW

Pen & Sword
MILITARY

AN IMPRINT OF PEN & SWORD BOOKS LTD.
YORKSHIRE - PHILADELPHIA

First published in Australia in 2018 by Big Sky Publishing Pty Ltd as *The Hell Pits of Sendryu*

First published in Great Britain in 2018 by
Pen & Sword Military
An imprint of
Pen & Sword Books Ltd
Yorkshire - Philadelphia

ISBN 978 1 52674 010 6

Printed and bound in England
By TJ International LTD

Pen & Sword Books Ltd incorporates the Imprints of Pen & Sword Books Archaeology, Atlas, Aviation, Battleground, Discovery, Family History, History, Maritime, Military, Naval, Politics, Railways, Select, Transport, True Crime, Fiction, Frontline Books, Leo Cooper, Praetorian Press, Seaforth Publishing, Wharncliffe and White Owl.

For a complete list of Pen & Sword titles please contact

PEN & SWORD BOOKS LIMITED
47 Church Street, Barnsley, South Yorkshire, S70 2AS, England
E-mail: enquiries@pen-and-sword.co.uk
Website: www.pen-and-sword.co.uk

or

PEN AND SWORD BOOKS
1950 Lawrence Rd, Havertown, PA 19083, USA
E-mail: Uspen-and-sword@casematepublishers.com
Website: www.penandswordbooks.com

CONTENTS

AUTHOR'S NOTE

ANGRY, argumentative, a living skeleton – that was the Jim Bodero I met 27 years after the war had ended. I'd just taken over as editor of the newspaper where he was a compositor/reader, the scourge of any journalist who mutilated the English language.

I understood his irascibility when I learned of the terrifying ordeals he'd been through as a prisoner of the Japanese, ordeals that for 27 years had left him in constant agony from a multiplicity of injuries.

He was a bitter man, not towards the Japanese who had caused his injuries, but towards Australian officialdom. Never out of pain from his damaged back and limbs, eyesight partially lost from a scarred cornea, Jim Bodero had his post-war claims for a Repatriation pension rejected.

Twenty years after the war ended, he aggravated the injuries to his back while working, but was refused workers' compensation by the insurance doctors, who said the injury was pre-existing. Of course it was pre-existing, the Japanese guards had seen to that.

Yet in contrast to Australia's denial, the Japanese had paid him compensation when he was nearly blinded while working down a coalmine in their country.

I often offered to write about his experiences, but he always refused, saying he didn't want to talk about the war. Then one day he asked me to tell his story.

When I started writing it, I was surprised by the extent of his memory. He was able to recall names, places, dates and incidents with vivid clarity.

We met only when he was well enough, and it took me the best part of twelve months before I had his story down on paper. I had just finished when I received a phone call. Jim Bodero was dead.

It was strange that after refusing me for so long, he had asked for his story to be told, strange also that he should have lasted just long enough for it to be completed.

CHAPTER ONE

THE FALL OF SINGAPORE

BANKNOTES, hundreds of them in all denominations, littered the street. Australian boots were trampling them into the dust but no one stopped to pick up the money. The men knew they'd get a vicious jab from a Japanese rifle butt if they so much as faltered on the march to Changi Prison.

The money was no good, anyway. It was Straits Settlement dollars, worth nothing now that Singapore had fallen. Looters had thrown it away.

Still, it had Sol Heffernan drooling. 'I might just do up me bootlace and pick up a motza–enough to retire to the south of France with a randy blonde for company.'

Trying to keep in step alongside him, Jim Bodero whispered that it'd be a bloody silly move. 'The stuff's not worth the paper it's printed on.'

'I know that, but I've never been close to so much dosh in all me life.' Sol took a kick at a thick bundle. It flew into the air and banknotes fluttered to the ground like outsize confetti. 'A six-pointer!' he yelled, remembering the time when he was scoring goals as the full-forward for Collingwood.

A jab in the ribs from a rifle butt knocked him off his feet. He fell in the dirt among the banknotes and other debris of war.

His mates marched on. They knew better than to stop to help him.

The guard raised his rifle above Sol's head. The marchers, looking back, despaired for him, but Sol's skull wasn't smashed in. The rifle was held menacingly until he struggled to his feet and staggered after the others.

The march continued as if nothing had happened. In the gutter, an executed man's head, severed by a Japanese sword and impaled on a pole, displayed a death grimace as if amused at the proceedings.

The men of C Company 2/26 Battalion had been in Singapore for a week when they were captured. Singapore, the last bastion after the failure to stop the Japanese advance down the Malayan Peninsula, was regarded as impregnable.

Together with the 2/29 and 2/30 battalions, and under direct control of the British Malayan Command, the men had crossed the causeway to Kranji on the island's northern coast and dug in. They could see hordes of Japanese massing in Johore, arrogantly making no attempt to conceal themselves. This contempt riled the Australians, who submitted repeated requests for permission to shell the enemy positions, but the British garrison brass refused.

One frustrated Australian artillery officer decided to do it anyway, and had his gun crews fire several shells. They didn't cause much damage, but the sight of the Japanese scurrying for cover was a boost to morale.

The British Malayan Command was ready to court martial the Australian officer for his breach of its orders, and he only avoided this fate because the imminent attack kept them too busy.

Enemy planes and observation balloons, secure in the knowledge they had no aerial opposition, filled the skies above the Australians' dug-in positions. In their slit trenches, two men to a trench, company platoons waited for the onslaught. Jim Bodero and Peter Murphy reinforced the roofing of their trench with heavy sleepers ripped up from the railway line.

The Japanese started a selective program of artillery harassment. Over an hour or more, they'd land hundreds of heavy rounds on a position, and then switch their attention to another, then another. They had ample ammunition, while the defenders had to conserve theirs.

The dug-in troops, expecting a full-scale attack to come at night, were particularly vigilant after dusk, but in daylight they relaxed sufficiently for inveterate gambler Peter Murphy to organise poker games in the Company Command building, a large, well-reinforced structure in a central position.

Play was often interrupted by fierce enemy shelling. When this happened, the cards were forgotten in the mad rush to get back to the slit trenches. In one of the hurried evacuations, Peter Murphy tried unsuccessfully to bar the exit, calling them a pack of dingoes for letting a few shells interrupt the game. It wasn't until the barrage eased and players drifted back to the game that Peter told them, 'I was holding the only decent hand I'd had all day and you pikers pissed off.'

'And we thought you were being courageous', one of his mates said.

There was another quick evacuation from a poker game when Jimmy Smith, the platoon truck driver, appeared in the doorway with an unexploded Japanese shell cradled in his arms.

This time Peter Murphy led the hurried exit.

Jimmy yelled at their departing backs, 'The writing on it says it was made by the Brisbane City Council.'

Curiosity stopped the fleeing men. Everyone knew the pig iron Australia had sent to Japan pre-war could be what was being fired at them, but a local government council back home making shells for Japan was real treachery.

They cautiously approached Jimmy, keen to see the evidence. Jimmy was grinning now. 'There's nothing about the Brisbane City Council. I just made that up.' He waved the live shell in the air, and everybody ducked. 'I just wanted to know what I should do with this thing.'

Given that the suggestions that were forthcoming were physical impossibilities, Jimmy left with his unexploded shell, apparently with the aim of frightening the shit out of someone else.

By now the Japanese were strafing and bombing from the air without resistance. Their heavy artillery barrages were causing devastation and receiving little reply from guns that were short of ammunition.

Confident of their superiority, the Japanese made repeated attempts to swarm into the Australian sector, but each attack was repelled.

They then switched their attention to the island's east and west coasts, where the defenders crumbled under the weight of enemy numbers.

The forces in the northern sector, now cut off from Singapore at the rear, were ordered to evacuate. With all motor transport out of action, the retreat was a footslog on roads clogged with civilians and uniformed personnel, all hurrying towards Singapore.

Huge oil storage tanks had been set on fire by the shelling and bombing, and columns of thick smoke from the burning oil billowed skywards.

It started to rain, and the oily soot in the air mixed with the rain to turn people black and grimy. Soon nobody could tell whether a person was friend or foe.

The Australians, ordered to rendezvous at the Singapore Botanical Gardens, had been given a compass course aimed at evading the encircling Japanese. They travelled on this until C Company's Pioneer section believed they were too far south-east, and should be heading more south-west. The main force decided to follow the original course, but the men of C Company opted to go their own way.

The original reading proved to be correct when the main force came to the pipeline that supplied water from Johore to Singapore. Following it, they ran into a party of Japanese and a battle ensued, only ending when the Japanese officer was killed and his troops disappeared in the jungle. The officer had made the mistake of climbing onto the pipeline and calling on the Australians to surrender, whereupon they shot him.

The force moved on to the assembly point at the Botanical Gardens. On arrival there, they were told that the Pioneer section that had followed its own compass course was missing.

Months later, a prisoner-of-war work party from Changi found their bodies. Spent .303 shells lying around the area indicated that the men hadn't died without a fight. When they had run out of ammunition, those who were still alive had been tied to trees and used for bayonet practice.

At the Botanical Gardens, the Australians were issued with a couple of tots of fiery Navy rum and ordered to attack a Japanese-held hill at Bukit Timah, on the outskirts of Singapore.

The Japanese were forced to retreat to a position behind another hill a short distance away across the valley. Though not far apart, neither side could see the other because of the hill in between. From close range, the Japanese laid down heavy shelling and mortaring.

The Australians dug in once more, two men to a slit trench. They had no artillery and could only reply to the fierce Japanese barrage with small-arms fire.

Japanese shells whined harmlessly over the Australian trenches, but mortar bombs were being lobbed over the hill with deadly accuracy.

The Australians were hungry. They hadn't been issued with rations for days and their only food had been whatever they could find in houses deserted by British officers of the Singapore garrison. In their hurry to get away, the British had left behind most of their possessions.

In one shell-pocked Bukit Timah house, the men found a steak-and-kidney pie. It was in a refrigerator rendered useless after Singapore's electricity supply was knocked out. Without refrigeration, it had turned green and its pastry was like a block of cement, but to hungry men, it represented food.

Peter Murphy, always the planner, decided to make a decent meal with the pie as the main course. For an entrée, he'd serve puftaloon scones, made from flour he'd found in the pantry. He remembered these doughy lumps of damper being a staple item in the hungry days of Australia's Great Depression.

However, he struck trouble when he went to cook the scones and heat the pie. The gas stove in the house was as useless as the refrigerator. Gas, like electricity, was no longer available, so Peter lit a fire on the floor.

The smoke that rose from it was seen by the Japanese observation balloons, and their artillery opened up. The men ignored the shrapnel whistling around them as they ate their mouldy pie and doughy puftaloons.

For after-dinner drinks, the men had the finest Hennessy brandy. The British officer who had fled the house had left a cellar filled with cases of the best spirits and liquors. As they ate, Peter Murphy raised his mug and toasted the British army for looking after its garrison officers so well.

A search of the house revealed that it had been used for gambling parties. Peter confiscated a roulette wheel, which he said would make a change from poker to while away the time between shellings.

The gambling devices and well-furnished rooms were an indication of the life of luxury the British garrison officers had been living, confident in the belief that Singapore was safe from attack. Huge fifteen-inch naval guns capable of hurling one-ton projectiles miles out to sea, supported by batteries of nine-inch guns, were regarded as sufficient to repel any enemy intent on entering the harbour.

However, the wily Japanese didn't come by sea. They knew Singapore's guns faced seawards in fixed positions and could traverse only a hundred and eighty degrees. The harbour might be secure, but in the other direction, the Malayan mainland was an open back door. Hence, the Japanese came through the back door, and the British garrison forces were trapped.

When the water supply from Johore Bahru on the mainland was cut, the garrison was in desperate trouble. The Malayan Command ordered it to hold out a little longer, stating that relief was on the way. Large forces of Americans were coming, it said. Soon the skies would be black with Allied planes.

The planes did come, Spitfires and Hurricanes. One count put the figure at a hundred, but the planes never made it into the air. The fuselages arrived in Singapore, but the engines remained in Java, still in their crates.

'What a cock-up that was', Peter Murphy said now as the conversation changed from food to the desperate position they were in with shells whistling above their Bukit Timah slit trench, too shallow to offer much protection.

Peter brought out the roulette wheel he'd confiscated from the pie-and-puftaloons house. He couldn't resist gambling, though when he bet he usually lost, and was always dead broke. 'If it was raining five-pound notes, I'd pick up a summons', he'd say.

In their current predicament, a shallow slit trench was no place for an unlucky gambler. When Jim saw Peter blowing air skywards as he toyed with the roulette wheel, he thought it was some strange gambling superstition.

Finally, he had to ask. 'Peter, what are you doing?'

'I'm creating an updraft.'

'What for?'

'It's a known fact that the course of a shell can be changed if it hits an updraft of air.' Peter continued to blow.

Jim shook his head in disbelief, but Peter's method seemed to work because the shells kept passing overhead.

At about five o'clock the following afternoon the two men were still crouched in the trench when the shelling stopped, as did the mortar bombing. A strange silence settled over the scene.

From across the valley came frenzied Japanese shouting. 'Banzai! Banzai!'

This is it, the Australians told each other, and prepared for a massive attack, but the attack didn't come. At seven o'clock that night, 15 February 1942, they learned why.

The defenders of Singapore had surrendered.

CHAPTER TWO
CHANGI PRISON

THE Australians were told by their officers to lay down their arms and stay in their positions until morning. Then, they would be marched to a padang, a Malayan recreation ground, where they would become prisoners of the Japanese army.

The men were in a state of shock. They'd never imagined this could happen. The situation was desperate, but surrender was unthinkable. They couldn't believe the Malayan Command had given in.

The rest of the night was spent speculating about what the future would hold as captives of the Japanese. They had no idea what to expect. Stories were rife of atrocities the Japanese had committed against civilians during their advance down the mainland. Word had not yet filtered through that by way of retribution for the cost of the Malayan campaign-the Japanese had lost more dead than the entire number of Allied troops defending the territory-they had murdered the doctors and nurses in a Singapore hospital and bayoneted the wounded as they lay helpless in their beds.

About three thousand Australian troops from the 2/26, 2/29 and 2/30 battalions were herded into the Singapore padang for the surrender. Armed Japanese milled about, seemingly doing their best to appear friendly. They walked among the captives, smiling and nodding to them.

'Get onto this bloke', Sol Heffernan nudged. A short rotund Japanese soldier had brought a mouth-organ out of his pocket. 'I think he's going to give us a concert.'

The Japanese man started playing, not some patriotic song of Nippon, but *Auld Lang Syne*.

The men were hushed as the strains of the sentimental ballad reminded them of home and their families.

It was a friendly enough scene for Sol to make a remark that was soon to prove to be a badly misplaced piece of optimism. 'Doesn't look as if we're going to have much trouble getting on with this mob.'

On the fifteen-mile march to Changi, when he received a rifle butt in the ribs for his dropkick at the worthless money, he admitted he could be wrong.

By the time the weakened men reached Changi, they were exhausted and showing the effects of the beatings they'd received along the way.

Changi Prison's main buildings were concrete, three storeys high, and had been badly damaged by aerial bombing and shellfire. Beneath one of the buildings lay an unexploded five-hundred-pound bomb.

When the Australians arrived at the jail, the civilian prisoners it housed were moved into what had been the barracks of the Scottish regiment, the Gordon Highlanders, before Singapore fell.

The prison had no barricades, so the Japanese ordered the men to make it secure. Around the perimeter, they were forced to build three rows of triple dannett, a circular tunnel of barbed wire. Two of the rows were side by side, and the third was on top of them. Alongside this was a row of double apron-four strands of barbed wire close together with an apron down each side. For extra security, another three rows of triple dannett were added.

Sol made another incorrect observation when the barricades were finished. 'A man'd have to be a bloody snake to get through this.'

It wasn't long before the wire was being breached at night, not by snakes, but by desperately hungry prisoners. The daily ration was just a handful of rice and an Indian army biscuit with a small piece of cheese or sardine on it. Some of the rice had been sprinkled with lime to combat weevils and when cooked, it turned yellowish-green and had a vile taste.

Despite this meagre diet, the weakened prisoners were forced to do heavy work outside the compound, mainly unloading ships in Singapore harbour and cutting wood for the cooking fires.

Nobody tried to avoid the harbour work because it provided a chance to scrounge a few grains of rice or a tin of jam or milk from the ships' crews. Anything they were given had to be smuggled back into the prison. If they were caught, it meant a bashing or worse from the Japanese guards.

Grisly sights were common for the work parties. One group was given the job of burying the decaying Chinese corpses that were strewn along a Changi beach. They'd been marched into the water and machine-gunned. The Japanese had expected the tide would carry the bodies out to sea, but instead it had pushed them up onto the sand.

Machine-gunning in the water was an execution method the Japanese were to use later on Australian nurses in Sumatra.

Another work party on clean-up duty found a tarpaulin-covered pile from which came the putrid smell of rotting flesh. When the guards used their rifle butts to keep them away from seeing what the pile contained, the men feared it was more bodies.

One prisoner managed to get close enough to sneak a look under the tarpaulin. He saw dozens of corpses in an advanced stage of decomposition. However, these were not Allied bodies; they all wore the navy blue uniform of the Japanese Imperial Guard, a crack division operating in the Malayan campaign. The bodies were apparently awaiting cremation, the Japanese way of disposing of their dead.

Instead of grieving over another atrocity, the prisoners were relieved to find that this time, the death pile was the enemy.

With many thousands of Changi prisoners confined to an area about the size of an average town shopping block, there was always the danger of an outbreak of disease. Latrines were carefully constructed, and all waste was sedulously disposed of to guard against germ-carrying flies. Hundreds of deep holes were dug to cater for the large number of men, and they were constantly being filled in and new ones dug.

Time was filled in at night with the 'group natter', a prisoners' talkfest wherein the main topics were food and how long it would take the Allies to turn the tide of the war and release them from captivity. Some estimated it would be all over in a few weeks, a few months at the most. Most, though, thought it would take at least a year.

Jim Bodero was pessimistic. He knew the task was formidable. In Europe and the Pacific, Germany and Japan had swept all before them, and it would take a supreme effort to halt the momentum, let alone turn the tide. He predicted to the group that 'By the time this stoush is over, those of us who are still around will be much older, and we'll have changed so much we'll be hard to recognise.'

Using a stub of pencil and a scrap of paper, in April 1942 he wrote a verse on the outcome of the war. He was to carry it with him for three and a half years.

We'd won, and everywhere the flags were flying
Proudly, gaily fluttering in the breeze,
Pennants brave of many different colours,
Commemorating famous victories.
The cities' streets were thronged with people
To welcome home their heroes from the war,
Triumphal arches, streamers and confetti,
As they had some twenty years before,
And as they will some twenty years later.
For man's a creature strange, without much wit,
And each great war becomes a little greater
Than the great war previous to it.
They marched in threes past the civic building,
Where midst a mass of braid and medals bright
His Ex, the governor-general of Australia,
Erect and proud, awaited the 'eyes right'.
Accompanied by strains of martial music
Marched to shouts and cheers, 'Six' and 'Seven'
Then came the Eighth . . .
His Ex's eyebrows twitched towards the heavens,
'I will admit,' he said to those about him,
'Times have changed tremendously of late,
But of one thing I really am most certain,
There's more than that belong to Number Eight.'
The Chief of Staff agreed with this assertion,
And from a group of laurel wreaths and crowns
Called his trusted deputy towards him
To probe the pros and cons and ups and downs.
The deputy was really most resourceful,
His deputy he sent for interview,
And so on till they found within the army
A deputising deputy who knew.
He hastened to report upon the matter,

That insomuch as far as he could say,
According to the latest information,
The missing men had not yet left Malay.
He'd written airmail on the 13th instant
Informing them the armistice was signed,
With instructions to report back to Australia
Just as soon as everyone had felt inclined.
Just then there came a noise of much excitement
And people moving down towards the shore,
For queer boats of many shapes and sizes
Were quietly floating inward by the score.
Soon they beached, and climbing from the sampans,
For such these craft had since turned out to be,
There came a motley crowd of human beings
Like bits of jetsam cast up by the sea.
Silently the crowd gave way before them
As they staggered out on to the beach,
Never was there beheld such a procession,
Or ever seen a shambles so complete.
Hair long and black, beards thick and flowing,
And teeth stained from the juice of betel nut,
Bodies clad in sarongs, towels and loincloths,
And faces browned and scarred with parang cuts.
Some led goats or monkeys there behind them,
And one rode on a water buffalo.
In the van were many brown-skinned children,
But who were whose no one seemed to know.
Still they struggled, staggering ever onwards,
Till at last no further could they go,
Exhausted, swooning, sank to earth there dying,
With a last despairing 'Ullo, Joe.'
They buried them midst peaceful scenes familiar,
Where all is still, save when the evening breeze
Is softly heard sometimes when gently stirring
Midst the coconut and rubber trees.

Some of the guards at Changi were Korean. Their Asian appearance had the Australians thinking they were Japanese, but the difference soon became apparent. The Koreans were bigger physically and packed a much harder wallop.

The Japanese were contemptuous of the Koreans and would punish them for little reason. Unable to retaliate, the Koreans took it out on the prisoners.

Their viciousness earned them nicknames. The most sadistic was called BB (for Boy Bastard), whose sadism was almost matched by BBC (Boy Bastard's Cobber).

The one called Dillinger had all the evil of the American gangster. He killed a prisoner by taking him outside the camp on some pretext and then shooting him, claiming he had been trying to escape. The dead man's mates knew it was murder, but they could do nothing about it.

Another Korean was called the Storm Trooper. Built like an ox, he could have shown his Nazi namesakes a thing or two about cruelty.

The prisoners regarded this foursome as the worst of the Korean guards, though others ran them pretty close. Rubber Chewer was given his name because when annoyed, he would grab a fistful of leaves from a rubber tree and chew them. Wart Eye's tag was a natural- he had masses of warts around his eyes. Blubber Lips' thick protruding lips flapped when he spoke, and Chindegar Jim was a runt who'd trade chindegar, a sweet substance made from the dried sap of the goola malacca tree, for a cup of burnt rice coffee.

The Australians had a reason for not calling any guard Ned Kelly. They said that bushranger Ned was a gentleman compared with this lot.

The Koreans were ever on the lookout for an excuse to inflict punishment. One of their favourite tactics was to sneak up on a work party, catch it unawares, and then bash the men because they didn't bow to them.

To counter this, a warning system was developed. If someone called out 'Red light, BB', it meant Boy Bastard was around. 'Red light, Storm Trooper' meant there was another very good reason to be wary. The warning relied on the belief that none of the Koreans spoke English. A few had a smattering of the language but pretended they didn't, hoping a prisoner would say something that would be worth a beating.

Anything of value the Australians had finished up in Korean pockets, traded for food, tobacco or money. As the men grew more hungry, items of great sentimental value such as going-away presents from their community back home were traded or sold. Watches and rings couldn't be eaten, but money obtained in this way was sneaked outside the wire and used to buy some morsel of food from the natives.

Always on the lookout for something to eat, Jim and Sol were in a woodcutting party pulling an old truck chassis loaded with timber when they heard animal squeals and grunts coming from some ramshackle buildings on a hill behind a stand of tall bamboo.

Jim couldn't believe his ears. 'Bloody pigs. I can hear bloody pigs. And pigs on the hoof mean roast pork and ham.'

Sol swallowed his drool. 'A pork chop would go down very nicely, thank you.'

It started Jim thinking. 'We could grab a porker if we got under the wire at night.'

'How do we get a live pig back under the wire into the compound?'

'Not under the wire. Over it. We'd have two blokes inside. The pig would be tossed to them. They'd catch it. The two who pinched it would sneak back under the wire.'

He took his idea back to the compound where his hungry mates were all in favour. Jim and fellow Queenslander Snowy Baker were appointed to commit the thievery, while Victorians Bill Haley and Sol would be the catchers.

Sol, the Aussie Rules player, was warned not to drop the pass.

'I'll be careful,' he said. 'The umpires might award a free kick.'

The night of the pig heist was dark. After the guards had made their two-hourly patrol, Jim and Snowy crawled under the wire. To get to the cover of the bamboo in front of the pigsty, they'd have to cross open ground that had only a few stumps and fallen branches for cover. That meant chancing being seen by the guards at a second compound that had been built separate from the main prison to hold those awaiting execution.

Dodging and weaving among the limited cover, the pair made it to the bamboo undetected. A gap in the clump of greenery was used by workers to get to the pigsty. The plan was for Snowy to wait there while Jim pilfered a pig, brought it back and tossed it to him. Snow would catch the pig, sneak it back to the prison and toss it over the wire to the waiting pair in the compound.

'Who said pigs can't fly', Snowy grinned.

Clutching the thick iron bar he'd christened his pig donger, Jim crawled towards the buildings, which were silent now. The pigs must be asleep. In the first pen, he saw fat porkers lying in the mud and manure. He rejected them as too big and heavy to carry. In another pen were several younger, smaller pigs. These would be more manageable. They woke when he crawled among them, but made no objection. It crossed Jim's mind that if pigs didn't object when he was near them, he could do with a good wash.

He slithered around before cornering a plump young porker. It got to its feet, seemingly stunned by the presence of a muck-covered human in its territory at night. It was stunned even further when Jim delivered a whack behind the ear with his pig donger.

With the unconscious pig cradled in his arms, he staggered back to the bamboo clump.

'Catch this', he whispered, throwing the pig through the gap to where Snowy waited.

'Got it', Snowy whispered back.

Then Jim got greedy. 'Take it back to the boys. I'm going to snaffle another one.'

He slithered back to the pigsty, where the animals had apparently noted what had happened to one of their kind and were no longer silent. They were running about squealing, making enough noise to wake the dead let alone a compound full of vicious guards. With no time to pick and choose, Jim made a wild swipe with the pig donger at a fat animal that stood squealing and eyeing him. The blow glanced off its snout, and the pig squealed even louder.

A couple more hefty whacks and the pig was down but not out. It struggled angrily and continued to protest as Jim carried it in his arms, unable to hurry because of the pig's size and objections.

Then all hell broke loose. Japanese shouting joined the pig squealing as three guards came charging out of the dark waving rifles with long bayonets attached.

Jim took off. In his heyday he'd won sprint races, but the recent restricted diet and the weight of the struggling pig took the edge off his speed. He was quickly run down by a guard. The Japanese was so close that Jim could almost touch the bayonet.

In desperation, he turned and threw the pig at his pursuer.

It hit the guard in the chest, and he went down with the angry porker kicking and squealing on top of him. The other two guards stopped in their tracks, probably not used to the sight of a Son of Nippon beneath a pig.

Jim didn't wait for them to recover. Pigless, he covered the distance to the bamboo in a time that would have done him justice in his sprint days. However, in the dark, he had no idea where the gap in the bamboo clump was. When he thought he was near it, he dived blindly. Fortunately, he couldn't have aimed better, and speared through the opening.

On the other side, he couldn't believe his eyes. Snowy was still there with the first pig.

Jim didn't have time to ask why. 'Japs!' he yelled. 'Go for your bloody life, Snow.'

Snowy dropped the pig and ran.

Jim wasn't about to let the pig go. He grabbed it by the hind legs and with it still kicking and squealing, he galloped the remaining distance over the open ground and threw it to the waiting catchers.

He'd lost sight of Snowy, but when he heard a loud crash some distance away, followed by the compound wire twanging and rattling, Jim's heart fell. It had to be Snowy running headlong into the wire in the dark. The noise would have brought the guards running, which would mean the end of Snowy.

Meanwhile, Jim had problems of his own. The three Japanese guards were close now, because he could see the light of their torches. With no time to get under the wire, he fell on his stomach among the sparse tree stumps and fallen timber and held his breath.

The guards were near enough for him to hear them speaking. He started to breathe again when they turned and went back the way they had come. It dawned on him that they'd heard the noise made by someone running into the wire, thought it was him and that he'd now been caught by the prison guards.

When they'd gone, Jim crawled under the wire, sick at heart to have been saved by Snowy's bad luck. Inside the compound, Sol and Bill were waiting, still holding the pig he'd thrown. They saw he was alone. 'Where's Snowy?' Sol asked.

Jim relayed the bad news. 'You must have heard the crash of Snow hitting the wire in the dark. The guards would have grabbed him for sure, poor bugger.'

'We heard the noise', Sol said. 'We thought the Nips had got both of you.'

They all fell silent. The death of a mate was a heavy price to pay for a pork meal.

Though his heart was as heavy as any, Jim snapped them out of the sad moment. 'Come on, you blokes. Snow wouldn't want us to stand around mourning him. He'd want us to get the pig out of sight before the Nips find us with it. Let's get it into the hut and hide it until we can knock it over.'

The inside of the hut was dark. The three men and the pig were feeling their way around when a voice said, 'Evening all.'

Jim lit a match. Snowy, whose body was covered in cuts and scratches, was lying on the sleeping platform smoking a cigarette.

Sol was the first to recover from the surprise. 'We thought the Nips got you. What happened?'

Snowy grinned. 'I hit the wire.'

'We know you hit the bloody wire. We heard it. Why aren't you dead?'

'I reckon I should be. I made enough noise to wake up every Jap between here and Tokyo, but the bastards must have been on the sake or something. Nobody came looking, so I decided to go to bed.'

'You went to bed!' Sol howled. 'And there's us smelling like pig shit thinking about where we'd plant you.'

Jim wanted to know why Snowy had stayed at the bamboo with the first pig when he was supposed to take it to the wire and toss it over.

'I didn't think you were much of a pig handler. Thought I'd stay and give you a hand with the second one.'

'*I'm* not much of a pig handler?' Jim snorted. 'Who was it dropped the first pig just because a few Japs were running around with fixed bayonets? If I hadn't picked it up, we'd have gone through all this for nothing.'

'All's well that ends well', Snowy said, settling back. 'When do we eat pork?'

The pig was slaughtered the next day, and with proper food in their stomachs, everyone agreed it had been worth all the trouble.

CHAPTER THREE
THE LARRIKIN

THE lanky frame, the unruly crop of wire-like black hair, the perpetual half-grin that seemed to be enjoying some private joke, meant that it could only be Tellamalie, the larrikin Jim hadn't seen since early training days. Nobody knew what his real name was. The Tellemalie tag had been hung on him because of the careless way he handled the truth, particularly when he needed to talk his way out of trouble. And Tellemalie was always in trouble.

But there he was now, among the sea of faces in the Changi compound.

Jim slapped him on the shoulder. 'Tellemalie! Last time I saw you was at Caloundra in 1940.'

The man wheeled around. 'Sorry mate, you've got the wrong bloke. The name's Jack Martin.'

'Come off it. You're Tellemalie. We were at the Caloundra camp together. Jim Bodero … remember?'

'You've made a blue. I ain't never seen you before in me life.'

'Hey, this is me you're talking to, Tellemalie. Don't give me that "Jack Martin" bullshit. And what's with that Mobile Laundry colour patch? When I last saw you in 1940 you were heading off to the Middle East with the 2/25th.'

The man held up his hands and looked around. 'All right, all right, you've sprung me. But don't talk so bloody loud.' Tellemalie drew him into a corner. 'It's like this.' He lowered his voice. 'The 2/25th didn't go to the Middle East. We got posted to Darwin as garrison troops. I joined this bloody army to see a bit of the world, and I wasn't going to be stuck in god-awful Darwin for the duration, so I start playing up … you know, making a bit of a bastard of meself.' He gave an impish grin. 'I can do that pretty well, as you might know. Anyhow, I figured if I played me cards right I'd get tossed out of the army up in Darwin. Then I'd re-enlist under another name and get a posting more to me liking.'

'So you got tossed out?'

'Nah, got tossed in. Into Darwin's Fanny Bay jail.'

'Into jail? What for?'

'It's a long story. I'll tell you about it someday. It wasn't so bad in Fanny Bay, easiest bloody slammer I've ever been in. They even let you out to cut the grass on the footpath and ask you if you'd mind coming back to jail later. Well, one day I forgot to go back. I went bush. Shit, mate, it's a long way from Darwin to Sydney. It took me months to get there. I walked, hitched rides, pinched horses, but I made it. In Sydney I joined up as Jack Martin.'

'So you got what you wanted-an overseas posting?'

'Got to go overseas all right', Tellemalie said. 'They stuck me in the Mobile-bloody-Laundry unit and sent me up here to bloody Singapore. Well, you don't think that was a bit of good timing. I arrived just in time for the Nips to grab me and stick me in this joint. Bloody sight worse than any of the clinks I've been in. The jail tucker was a hell of an improvement on what we get here.'

Jim couldn't help laughing. 'Never mind, Tellemalie, you wanted to see the world, and at least you're seeing something of Asia. And you can't get into too much trouble here.'

'Don't you believe it. Trouble's me second name. I get into trouble so often that if I was a sheila I'd never be out of the maternity hospital.'

'You ask for trouble, Tellemalie. What about the CO's horse at Caloundra?'

Tellemalie chuckled at the memory. 'I'll never forget the old bastard's face when he thought he was riding back to front.'

They laughed together at the memory. It had happened when the new CO, a stiff-backed colonel with a Pommy accent and a bristling white moustache, arrived for the first inspection of his men mounted on a prancing black horse. He dismounted and handed the reins to a sergeant, who passed them on to Tellemalie who was loafing nearby.

'Why give it to me, sarge?' Tellemalie complained. 'I don't know nothing about horses.' He held up the reins. 'I don't even know what this is called.'

The sergeant shook his head at such ignorance. 'They're the reins. And you don't have to know anything about horses to hold on to them. So start holding.'

'If I'm standing here holding on to these reins things and someone asks me something about the horse, I should be able to answer them, shouldn't I, sarge? How about giving me a few pointers?' He proceeded to ask what the various parts of the horse were. The sergeant patiently told him.

Tellemalie kept a straight face as he listened. He'd roped, saddled, broken and ridden more horses, including wild brumbies, than the sergeant had ever seen.

When he'd run out of parts to explain, the sergeant said, 'Do you understand about horses now?'

'I think so, sarge. Do they bite?'

'If this one bites, son, you're so raw it'll spit you out', the sergeant said, leaving Tellemalie grinning to himself.

As soon as the sergeant was out of sight, Tellemalie whipped the saddle off the colonel's horse and reversed it. An army saddle the wrong way round isn't easy to detect because the pommel and rear part of army saddles are about the same height. It becomes obvious only when the rider mounts and finds that the stirrups are at the horse's flanks instead of behind the front legs.

By the time the colonel returned to his horse, the sergeant was holding it again. He'd taken the reins from Tellemalie and told him to clear off. If anyone was going to get in the CO's good books for looking after his horse, it was going to be him.

The colonel mounted the horse and for a few seconds he just sat there, legs stretched out behind him like a motorbike rider. When he realised what was wrong, he roared at the sergeant, 'Are you trying to make me look like a fool? I'll have your stripes and you'll be peeling potatoes in the cookhouse!'

'Wasn't me, sir', the sergeant replied. 'It would have to be the private I had holding your horse. I took the reins off him when I saw you coming.'

'Who is this man? I'll make him wish he'd never joined the army.'

The sergeant was keen on self-preservation, but reluctant to dob in one of his men. He'd take care of Tellemalie later. 'He's new here, sir. One of a new batch of recruits. I wouldn't recognise him again.'

'I'll find out who he is', the colonel fumed. 'Everybody on parade. Immediately!'

When the troops were assembled before him, the colonel slapped his swagger stick against his thigh with menace. He could barely speak for anger. 'The private who switched the saddle on my horse will step forward.'

Nobody moved, least of all Tellemalie.

'I order you again. Step forward the guilty man.'

Again, there was no response.

'Then I regard every one of you as guilty!' the colonel shouted. 'You are all confined to barracks for a fortnight on extra duties.'

He turned and strode off the parade ground to his horse. With the saddle now placed the right way round, he was able to canter away sedately.

As they laughed about it now in Changi, Jim said, 'You were bloody lucky to get away with that one, Tellemalie.'

'I didn't exactly get away with it. The blokes gave me merry hell when they were confined to barracks, and the sarge gave me all the shit jobs around the place.'

'You seemed to be doing all right when you joined the unit's brass band.'

Tellemalie grinned. 'I'd almost forgotten about that.'

'How did you come to be in the band? Nobody knew you were musical.'

'I'm about as musical as an armless fiddler. I picked the band as a soft lurk when I saw them practising in the shade while everyone else was marching around in the hot sun.'

When he'd applied to join the band the interviewing officer had asked about his musical qualifications. 'He nearly had a fit when I told him I played the mouth organ, but I had him near tears when he heard about me deprived childhood and parents so poor they couldn't pay for me to have cornet lessons. All they could afford was a mouth organ.'

'And he let you join the brass band as a mouth organist?'

'Don't be bloody silly. Whoever heard of a mouth organ in a brass band. The officer sympathised with me about my deprived childhood. He found a cornet for me, told me to practise on it, and said I'd be in the band when I was good enough.'

Jim nodded. 'I remember you sitting in the shade with your cornet while we poor bloody footsloggers drilled and sweated.'

'Yeah, the band was a pretty easy touch.'

'So you finally learnt the cornet and made it into the band?'

'Nah. Never could get a note out of the bastard of a thing.'

Jim shook his head in admiration at the cheek of the man. 'Did they boot you out when they found out you couldn't play?'

'I gave it away. Turned in my cornet. If I'd stayed any longer they'd have wanted to make me bandmaster or something, so I applied for a job in the army stores.'

'The army stores?' Jim laughed. 'They used to say you should have been called Hydraulic Jack because you'd lift anything. Don't tell me you were able to talk your way into working where they keep all the expensive gear?'

Tellemalie shook his head sadly. 'I was rejected. Can't understand it, after I told them about my experience with stores.'

'You'd been a storeman?'

'Store bullocks. I'd rounded up plenty of stores in the outback.'

Bodero grinned. 'With all that experience, they didn't want you in their stores?'

'Shit, mate', Tellemalie said as he departed, 'the army's stupid, but not that stupid.'

Days later, when Jim ran into him in the compound, Tellemalie's tattered tunic no longer had the Mobile Laundry patch on the sleeve. Now it carried the colours of the 2/29 Battalion.

Jim pointed to the colour patch. 'Another regimental change?'

'Matter of self-preservation. I've been checking on which mob in this place is eating the best. Nobody's doing too well, but the 2/29 seems to be doing better than most, so I've put myself on battalion strength.'

'You can't just walk in like that, Tellemalie. They're going to wake up.'

'They wouldn't wake up if the roof fell in on them. In each company, there's a few blokes who know each other. The rest wouldn't know if bloody Hirohito was among them.'

That was the last Jim saw of Tellemalie in Changi. It was to be in another prisoner-of-war camp much later in the war that they were to meet again.

The Japanese knew prisoners were getting out of Changi at night and smuggling in food. Fred Ennett, a corporal from Mount Isa, was caught outside the wire. They beat him unmercifully, but Fred still smiled. It was a habitual smile-he didn't know he was doing it. When they couldn't wipe it off his face, the guards grew angrier and beat him harder, but the smile remained. Maddened, they took to him with clubs and fists, and then kicked him down a steep flight of concrete stairs. Fred died of his injuries.

Changi had many Sikh guards who had defected to the Japanese after the fall of Singapore. The Sikhs caught two prisoners climbing trees outside the wire in search of coconuts and handed them over to the Japanese. The two men were badly beaten.

However, the coconuts were nutritious, and it took more than a beating to discourage Jimmy Harris, a big cane farmer from Mackay. He was up a coconut palm one dark night when a Sikh guard came along and paused for a rest underneath him, his back against the trunk.

Although he was hidden by the palm fronds, Jimmy knew that if he moved he'd be heard, so he kept still, which allowed hordes of vicious yellow-and-green stinging ants to attack. Naked but for his torn shorts, Jimmy suffered in silence until the Sikh left and he was able to climb down. Jimmy was in great pain, but at least he had a couple of coconuts to eat. To a hungry man, that was a fair enough exchange.

Not long after that, he was with a work party outside the wire when he caught a sparrow. Only half-grown, the tiny bird couldn't fly properly. Still, it was food. Jimmy wrung its neck and was plucking the feathers when Bob Brennan, the sergeant in charge of the work party, saw what he was doing.

Brennan, a timber cutter from Maryborough in Queensland and the battalion's heavyweight boxing champion, was a renowned joker. 'You wouldn't eat that poor little sparrow, would you, Jimmy?' he said. 'It's only a baby.'

The work party knew he was having the bloke on, and stood by grinning.

Jimmy looked at the tiny lifeless body in his hand. 'You're right', he said, placing it gently on the ground. 'A man can't be that bloody hungry.'

He hadn't walked two paces from the dead bird before someone grabbed it and ate it raw.

Sparrows and most other creatures were fair game, although hard to find. Greens were just as scarce, and grass and the fleshy cabbage-like leaves from the tops of coconut palms served as vegetables. Obtaining the coconut cabbage was the most risky undertaking. The tree had to be cut down, and that brought the worst punishment if anyone was caught in the act.

The prisoners, desperate for greens, asked the Japanese for plants to start a vegetable garden inside the jail. The Japanese surprised them by providing not only plants, but a bag of blood-and-bone fertiliser.

Sol Heffernan and Jim Bodero opened the bag.

Sol smelt it. 'Hey, that's not too bad.'

Jim had a sniff. 'Smells like shit.'

'Says on the bag it's blood and bone. Blood comes from animals, so does bone. And animals are food, ain't they?'

'Still smells like shit.'

'Well, I say it's tucker. And we're not going to waste tucker on a bloody garden.'

'What do you reckon we do with it?'

'We eat it', Sol said.

'We can't eat fertiliser.'

'Not straight out of the bag. We'll make fertiliser rissoles.'

Sol emptied the contents out of the bag, added water, patted the mixture into small, round rissoles and cooked them on the open fire. He took the first bite.

'What's it like?' Jim asked.

Sol stopped trying to chew. 'If ever I get home, never again will I criticise the missus's cooking.'

Sol never made it home. Married a few weeks before he embarked for Malaya, he didn't get the chance to sample his wife's cooking again. He was drowned with hundreds of other prisoners off the Philippines in 1944 when an American submarine sank the ship carrying them to Japan to work as slaves. But that was to happen much later. Now, as they tested their tortured digestion with fertiliser rissoles, they couldn't have imagined what lay ahead of them.

The garden did pretty well without fertiliser, but the prisoners were never to taste what it grew. It was looking promising when the Japanese suddenly announced that they wanted a workforce to go to Burma.

'Much better in Burma', they told the prisoners. 'Plenty food, plenty medicine.' They even hinted that the men might be repatriated in exchange for Japanese prisoners of war.

The Australians had been in Changi from the end of February 1942 to the beginning of May. Deciding that nothing could be much worse, many of the men were ready to volunteer to go to Burma, but they weren't given the chance-they were detailed to go by their officers.

In the A-Force detachment, Jim and Snowy Baker were with nearly a thousand others, including Peter Murphy, Jimmy Harris, Johnny Gorman, Dickie Barnes and Sol Heffernan.

Johnny Gorman, a dusky South Sea islander, lived at Mackay in north Queensland. The first Japanese he met as a prisoner of war poked a finger in his chest and asked, 'Who you?'

'I'm an Aussie', Johnny told him proudly.

'No, no', the Jap said. 'Australian white, not black.'

Johnny was to come up against this throughout his imprisonment. The Japanese had trouble understanding that black people could be Australians.

Johnny was among those who lost their lives towards the end of 1944 when the ship taking prisoners to Japan was torpedoed.

Dickie Barnes, a corporal and section leader, was more than sixty years of age. He was a First World War veteran who carried a souvenir of the war, a huge hole in his right buttock from a machine-gun burst. How he came to be in the Second AIF at his age was a mystery, because the maximum enlistment age at the time was thirty-nine.

Dickie had spent most of his life working on sheep stations in outback Queensland. The day he enlisted, he kicked the last sheep down the race and said, 'I hope I never see another of you woolly bastards in my lifetime.'

He was to see many more of them, however, because Dickie survived the war and returned to the outback sheep stations.

Based on his experiences in two wars, he didn't think much of the Second AIF compared with the Light Horse he'd served with in Palestine in the First World War. In comparison, the new breed of soldier was a Girl Guide, Dickie said.

He was on his way to Malaya with the Second AIF when the troopship called in for a stopover at Fremantle. During shore leave, Dickie's mates waited outside while he went into a well-known house in Rose Street. He was in there so long that they started to worry.

'He's only a little bloke', Snowy Baker said. 'He might have fallen in.'

When Dickie finally appeared, the others wanted to know what had kept him.

He looked embarrassed. 'I had trouble ... you know ... performing.'

'Haw, haw', Sol Heffernan roared. 'You couldn't get it up!'

'She was very helpful', Dickie said sadly, 'but it was mission impossible.'

'Maybe you should join the Girl Guides', Sol told him.

CHAPTER FOUR

MELBOURNE CUP 1942

THE men who were being sent to Burma and thought conditions couldn't be much worse than those in Changi found how wrong they were before they even arrived. Five hundred men, half of A-Force, were crowded into the hold of an ancient Japanese transport ship, the *Toyahashi Maru*. The other five hundred had boarded another ship.

The *Toyahashi Maru*, which was so badly rusted that a finger could be poked through its side, had been used to carry cavalry horses from Japan to Burma. The ship's hold was now covered in their dung.

The five hundred men were packed into the hold so tightly they could only stand or squat. Lying down was an impossibility. Bladders and bowels had to be evacuated where they stood. It was unbearably hot and the stench was overpowering. Within days, sweat swished around the hold, mixing with horse manure and human faeces and urine.

The daily ration was a small portion of cooked rice and a cup of water.

One day, a Japanese sailor emptied a couple of cornsacks of tiny bread rolls into the hold. Rock hard and close to six weeks old, they were blue with mildew and covered in a hairy fungus. Even so, the desperately hungry men fought over them.

When the prisoners started to collapse and die in the stifling, stinking hold, the Australian officers were able to persuade the Japanese to allow a few on deck at a time, but they barely had enough time to fill their lungs with fresh air before they were forced back down into the hellhole.

The brief time on deck was used by some of the prisoners to sabotage the ship's gun. They took out the breech block and threw it overboard, knowing that the ship was now defenceless and any attack could have disastrous consequences for them. However, they figured it would be worth it just to see the Japanese trying to use the gun.

The *Toyahashi Maru* was at sea for three days before it reached its first port of call, Sumatra. It stayed there for a day refuelling, but the suffering prisoners remained locked in the hold. After what for them seemed an interminable time, the ship finally sailed again and was at sea for another three days before arriving at Victoria Point in lower Burma, where two hundred prisoners were taken off.

The ship then sailed further north to Mergui. Another two hundred were disembarked there, Jim Bodero and his mates among them.

Mergui was upriver, where it was too shallow for the *Toyahashi Maru*, so the ship anchored at the mouth of the river, far from the town. After unloading its suffering human cargo, the ship headed north to Tavoy with the remainder of A-Force, including Colonel Ramsay, who had been in overall charge. Those left at Mergui and Victoria Point were placed under the command of officers of lesser rank.

It was June 1942, and the prisoners who'd landed at the river mouth were exhausted and dehydrated from starvation and the privations of the terrible voyage. Nonetheless, they were forced to undertake the long march to Mergui. Many collapsed on the way, and were left where they fell. Surprisingly, these men later turned up at Mergui. The Japanese, in a rare display of compassion, had allowed them to rest and resume the march when they had recovered sufficiently.

At Mergui, work parties were formed. Some were allotted to the aerodrome, some to road-making, and others to the waterfront to unload the small boats and barges bringing supplies from larger ships anchored downstream.

A particularly distasteful job for the aerodrome workers was knapping, cracking huge chunks of blue metal into small pieces to be laid on the runways. This was done with a three-pound hammer. The constant pounding of hammer on stone left the men's arms aching badly. It was dangerous, too. Flying chips of blue metal dug into bare flesh and brought a constant fear of being blinded.

Hundreds of Burmese civilians worked alongside the prisoners. They had a way of showing their disapproval when the Japanese demanded more effort. Using their hammers in perfect unison, they'd set up a rhythmic beat that sounded as if work was going on, though not one scrap of blue metal was being cracked. When the beat lost its rhythm, the protest was over.

The Australian prisoners tried to copy it, but they could never match the perfect timing of the natives.

Alongside Bodero at the stone-knapping one day, the big South Australian Bill Finch managed to annoy a Japanese guard. The guard, who was short and plump, stretched up on tiptoes as he swung a soft drink bottle at Finch, who towered above him. The height discrepancy meant the bottle missed by some distance. The guard, realising that Finch's head was out of reach, kicked him in the shins. The lanky Australian yelped, bent over and rubbed his sore leg. Now more accessible, Finch's head copped a hit with the bottle.

When he saw that there wasn't much damage, Jim couldn't help laughing at the pantomime.

'What's so bloody funny?' Finch howled, rubbing both his head and his shin.

'I've heard of big blokes being cut down to size', Bodero said, 'but that's the first time I've seen it happen.'

While everybody tried to avoid the stone-knapping job, work on the waterfront was eagerly sought. There was always the chance of finding some tinned food or dried fish among the cargo, not to mention the chance of sabotaging the Japanese war effort.

Those who were unloading bitumen for the airfield managed the latter. Required to roll the large drums from a barge onto the wharf, they'd wait until a gap opened up between the barge and the wharf, and when it did, they'd roll the drum and it would disappear into the river. This always brought a bashing from the guards, but the prisoners regarded that as a small price to pay.

Bags of cement and lime were the least popular cargo to unload, as the dust caked the men's sweaty bodies and stung their eyes. However, the bags presented an ideal place to hide any food the prisoners were able to get hold of.

One day, they had a few tins of scrounged salmon hidden among the bags that a crane was unloading onto the wharf from a small launch when the combined weight of the crane and its load tilted the launch. As it leaned over, the Australian crane driver swung the loaded sling into its mast. The launch turned turtle and sank, disappearing into the muddy water and taking with it the crane, the cargo of cement and lime, the men in the unloading party and, worst of all, the tins of salmon hidden among the bags.

After a while, a few bubbles appeared, and then assorted heads broke the surface. Even losing pilfered food was considered acceptable if it meant that an exercise in sabotage had been successful.

Anything obtained on the wharves was smuggled back into camp by a variety of means. Hiding it under a slouch hat fell out of favour when the Japanese started hitting prisoners over the head to see if their hat contained anything. Secreting goods in the crotch of one's trousers could be painful, and there was always the danger that the funny walk would alert the guards. Armpits were sometimes used, but because few prisoners had a shirt to provide cover, this method had to be abandoned. Still, scroungers never stopped dreaming up new ways of hiding things.

The pilfered food allayed some of the hunger, but continuing starvation, disease and exhaustion were taking their toll. The bodies of those who died were taken to the local cemetery in a Burmese 'boong' cart dragged by fellow prisoners, who also dug the graves and performed the last rites.

The cemetery wasn't overlooked in the ongoing efforts to scrounge something to eat. The prisoners took rice, eggs, fruit, rice cakes and dried fish from Burmese graves that had been adorned with joss sticks and flowers to sustain the departed Burmese on their last journey to paradise. Rather than serving as a tribute to the dead, the food played a far more practical role in keeping Australian prisoners alive. The Burmese knew it was happening, but once they had carried out their obligations to their departed, they accepted the disappearance of food from the graves.

The Burmese had no love for the Japanese, even though at first they had welcomed them and their Greater East Asian Co-prosperity Scheme, touted as being for the benefit of all Asiatics under the protection and guidance of the Divine Emperor.

When that prospect turned sour, the people of Burma began to wish for the return of the British, even though they had no reason to love them either.

Food was scarce at Mergui, but shelter was adequate. The prisoners lived in solid wooden buildings that had been used as barracks by the British. Around these was a high wooden paling fence the Japanese thought would keep the prisoners confined, but they were mistaken. The men were getting out as regularly as they had in Changi. However, there was no wire to crawl under here. The way out was by latrine trench.

Dug in a corner of the compound, the long, deep trench had numerous logs across it, placed close together so the prisoners could squat over them. At one end of the trench, the men had built a narrow hidden platform just above the bottom of the trench. From here, a tunnel had been dug that ran under the fence and emerged in the dense jungle outside.

The latrine stank, and was crawling with flies and maggots. The Japanese wouldn't go near it, and that left the prisoners free to use the tunnel to come and go as they liked.

Outside the camp, Jim Bodero met a Burmese doctor, his wife and two young daughters. They took him into their house, gave him a meal, and as he ate, one of the daughters, a talented violinist, played for him. Being treated like a civilised person hadn't happened for so long that he had almost forgotten what it was like.

The friendship was brief, however, brought to an end when the Japanese caught a party of foragers outside the prison and found the tunnel. The men were given a summary trial and sentenced to death for trying to escape.

The Australian officers pleaded that they were not trying to escape, but merely looking for food, although the Japanese refused to reconsider, and said the sentence would stand.

A week later, the aerodrome work party saw a truck go past carrying the condemned prisoners. The men were all singing. As they passed, their mates saluted them. At the perimeter of the aerodrome landing area, not far from the work party, the truck stopped. The Japanese mounted their machine guns while the prisoners dug their own graves.

The work party watched in horror as the machine guns opened up.

Soon afterwards, a car arrived. In it was a Japanese officer and the Australians' camp medical officer, Colonel Tom Hamilton, who had to certify that the execution had taken place.

Afterwards, the Japanese vowed that a similar fate awaited any other prisoners found outside the camp.

Colonel Hamilton told the men that the death penalty was too heavy a price to pay for their foraging, and ordered them to stop. Not everybody did, but there were no more large-scale operations.

At Mergui, the Australians came into contact with a different type of Japanese. These were kaigun (sailors) whose ship had been sunk in the Indian Ocean. They'd been brought to Mergui to act as guards while they awaited placement on another ship.

The kaigun hated the heitai (soldiers). 'Japanese kaigun ichi ban, Japanese heitai dame dame (Japanese sailor number one, Japanese soldier no good)', the sailors told the prisoners.

The Australians never missed an opportunity to use this dislike to turn the Japanese against each other.

The heitai would march the work parties out to the aerodrome and hand over to the kaigun, who had a smattering of English. They also had an entirely different attitude to the war and their enemy. They encouraged the Australians to do as little work as possible and often joined them in foraging for food, some of which was brought by natives to the aerodrome perimeter under cover of the jungle.

However, although the prisoners liked the sailors, they were still the enemy, and it was their job to get rid of them if possible. An opportunity arose when a few sticks of gelignite and some fuses were uncovered while they were clearing rubbish from under the sailors' quarters. They set the explosives under the house, and planned to sneak back around midnight to light the fuse, but the plan had to be abandoned when no detonators could be found. Without detonators, the explosives were useless. While this saved the Japanese sailors, it probably saved the prisoners too. Had they carried out their plan, many of them would have been executed.

Orders came through in July 1942 stating that the prisoners were to leave Mergui and move north to Tavoy, where the whole of A-Force would be together once more.

The camp at Tavoy had been a Burmese school. It comprised a large two-storey concrete building that had been used for the students and several high-blocked wooden houses where the teachers and their families had lived. The shelter was better than anything previously provided, but the addition of the Mergui contingent meant it was now overcrowded.

On their first day there, a work party was taken out to the aerodrome by truck. Before starting work, they were subjected to a pep talk by Captain Saito, the corpulent Japanese officer in charge of construction. Saito told them they were lucky to be alive. His generosity in allowing them to stay that way should be rewarded by working diligently and cheerfully. They should sing and whistle while they worked.

Sing and whistle? The Australians wondered whether they had at last come across a Japanese with a sense of humour.

Tavoy aerodrome was fully operational. Heavy bombers took off from there almost daily, heading north to bomb Allied targets on the India–Burma front. Some planes returned badly damaged. One just managed to reach the runway before the landing gear collapsed. It slewed sideways, skidded into the jungle, and smashed into some trees.

The Japanese had no mobile workshop, so they left the wreckage there. It was a bonanza for the prisoners, who stole whatever they could move. Pieces of aluminium from the fuselage were turned into dixies, billycans, plates and spoons. Some of the more enterprising prisoners fashioned matchbox covers onto which they scratched lurid etchings of naked women. These were popular with the Japanese, who bought them, but seldom paid.

Rubber hacked from the plane's tyres became thongs, held onto the feet by rope made from the bark of a tree. They were much prized by the prisoners, most of whom had long been without footwear. Thongs, which became a popular post-war Australian dress item, may have originated at Tavoy in the pieces scrounged from that wrecked Japanese plane.

Bodero wasn't really surprised when he found out that the leader of the Tavoy business enterprises was the irrepressible Tellemalie. He hadn't seen him since Changi.

Jim made a point of looking him up.

'You still seem to be doing all right, Tellemalie', he said.

Tellemalie nodded. 'Business hasn't been bad, but it'll turn bad if we can't get another Jap plane to crash. All the aluminium from the last one has been used up. If we can't get another plane wreck, we'll suffer a serious commercial downturn.'

Tellemalie decided to take things into his own hands. To hurry things along and to be first on the scene for bits and pieces when they became available, he'd stand on an embankment beside the runway, urging incoming planes to crash. Day after day he stood there, ignoring Japanese orders that no prisoner was allowed near the airstrip.

None of the planes would oblige, however, and Tellemalie grew increasingly frustrated. He would wave a battered Dutch army straw hat at the planes as they landed and shout, 'Crash, you bastard, crash!'

One day Tellemalie wasn't there, and they didn't see him again. His sudden disappearance convinced the other prisoners that his luck had finally run out. The Japanese had surely put an end to his crash routine.

With the wrecked plane now reduced to a skeletal frame, the prisoners turned their attention to the instruments. Some of the parts became two efficient short-wave wirelesses, one of which was hidden in a millet broom used to sweep out the Japanese headquarters. Each morning while the Australian officers met with the Japanese to be given the day's work party duties, a prisoner would be sweeping out the building. The Japanese suspected that the men had a wireless, but although they searched everywhere, they never thought of looking in the broom that was being used in their own headquarters.

A second wireless was built into a wooden stool on which an officer would sit with the Japanese for the daily briefing. Not one, but two, wirelesses were under the very noses of the Japanese, but they never found out.

The wirelesses picked up the BBC. This news was generally regarded as not very reliable, but at least it gave them something to talk about in the group natter.

One day, a Tavoy work party was out collecting timber for fencing when it came across a herd of goats. It was a situation made to order for hungry men. Both the goats and the prisoners were unguarded.

Jimmy Harris was appointed slaughterman. When he'd singled out a large black-and-white billygoat and had his mates surround it, Jimmy dived in and quickly had it upended and its throat cut.

Now they had a problem. If the guards saw them with the meat when they took it back, it would be going into Japanese cooking pots, not theirs. They'd lose the meat and gain a bashing.

However, the meat was successfully smuggled into camp wrapped in a tattered oilskin cape hidden among the fencing timber. That night, the prisoners' cooking pots were busy, with goat on the menu.

Native yaks, too, were fair game, so long as the owners weren't around. When one of these beasts wandered too close to a work party outside the aerodrome perimeter, Zac Watts, a grazier from Texas in south-west Queensland, pointed it out to the Japanese guard. 'Takusan meshi ichi ban (plenty number one food)', he told him. 'We catch.'

The guard disappeared and returned with a long length of rope. Zac made it into a lasso, handed the end to the guard and told him the yak was likely to take off when he lassoed it. 'You'll have to hold on to the end of the rope. Don't let go. If you do we'll lose the bugger.'

Zac expertly tossed the noose over the yak's head. At first, it didn't object, but when the rope tightened around its neck it took off. As instructed, the guard didn't let go of the rope, which meant he was dragged along by the stampeding animal, his short Japanese legs touching the ground only now and then.

The prisoners were as short of entertainment as they were of food, and this was the best entertainment they'd had in years. At first, they didn't know whether to barrack for the guard or the yak, but their stomachs won. 'Don't let the bastard go', they yelled at the flying Japanese, and groaned when he finally dropped the rope.

Not only was it the end of a great circus act, it was the end of their hopes for a yak stew.

The Burmese were prepared to barter for food, but the Australians had little to barter with. When word got around that a soda-water bottle of petrol was worth five rupees, the prisoners whose job it was to refuel the Japanese aircraft by hand-pumping petrol out of forty-four-gallon drums suddenly had access to a source of income. Many small bottles were filled when the guards weren't looking, and they found a ready market.

Bodero got greedy, figuring that a bigger container would bring bigger rewards. He found a one-gallon steel jerry can in one of the hangars and managed to fill it. He then arranged to meet a Burmese buyer that night outside the wire between nine and ten o'clock. Bodero arrived on time, but there was no sign of the Burmese. Unbeknown to Bodero, the buyer had been alerted that the Japanese guards were out and about that night looking for prisoners outside the wire, so he wasn't about to turn up.

Bodero was still waiting when, from out of the darkness, a guard screaming in Japanese charged at him with a fixed bayonet. He parried the bayonet thrust with the can of petrol and swung it wildly. It hit the guard in the forehead. He went down, blood streaming from a big gash.

Jim got rid of the guard's rifle by throwing it into a water tong, a Burmese well. The Japanese guard hadn't moved, although it wasn't clear if he was dead or merely unconscious. The bayonet thrust had slashed the can and petrol was leaking from it, so Jim threw it at the Japanese and ran for his life.

Back on his sleeping platform, he waited for the inevitable uproar. It didn't take long before the Japanese were rushing about with fixed bayonets shouting 'All men out! All men out!'

The prisoners were lined up, and a kempeitai officer, almost frantic with rage, told them a guard had been found unconscious and injured, with a can containing stolen petrol lying beside him. The attack on the guard could only have been made by a prisoner, and the guard's rifle was missing. 'If rifle here, we will find it', the officer fumed. 'Whoever did this will be punished. Very bad hitting guard, taking rifle.'

The prisoners were lined up and their building was searched. When no rifle was found, the men were ordered to hold out their hands to be examined for bayonet cuts and were smelt for any trace of petrol. The kempeitai had decided that no Japanese would allow his rifle and bayonet to be taken without at least inflicting some cuts, so petrol leaking from the slashed can would have left an incriminating smell on whoever had attacked the guard.

While the hand investigation went on, Bodero's mind was in turmoil. What would he do if one of his mates was found to have a fresh cut on his hand or had been handling petrol? Would he be man enough to confess, knowing he'd be executed?

Fortunately, he didn't have to make that decision. The kempeitai found no hand cuts and no smell of petrol, and left in anger.

However, the incident put an end to petrol pilfering. The guards, determined to catch someone, were now more alert during refuelling.

Bodero later told his mates what had happened, that he was the one responsible for the attack on the guard. They didn't thank him, though. He'd ruined the petrol-trading caper, which had been a useful income earner.

'Speedo! Speedo! Hyaku mena shigoto!' The Japanese guard wanted a work party of a hundred men in a hurry.

The chosen prisoners were loaded into trucks and taken to a cluster of jungle huts a couple of hundred yards apart. There, they were ordered to form a human chain and transfer British army mosquito nets, cases of tinned coffee and low-grade soap from one hut to another.

After the job was finished, the prisoners were taken back to the Tavoy camp, but had no time to rest. The kempeitai appeared and ordered everyone to line up beside their gear. A case of tinned coffee, three mosquito nets and seven cases of soap had been stolen.

The men were as guilty as hell, but they were confident the search wouldn't turn up any of the pilfered goods. They had been well-hidden in the jungle before the prisoners returned to camp.

When they were ordered to empty out their kitbags, a variety of items tumbled onto the floor, among them cameras, field glasses and compasses … even a revolver.

Possession of a firearm meant immediate death, but the single-minded Japanese weren't looking for guns. They were looking for coffee, mosquito nets and soap. When they didn't find any, they told the prisoners to put their gear away and left, but soon returned.

Apparently, what they'd seen falling from the kitbags had finally registered, and they ordered the kitbags to be emptied out again. However, by now, there was nothing to be found. The revolver and other illegal goods had quickly been hidden elsewhere.

Nevertheless, the guards did find a few lumps of soap. These hadn't come from the missing cases, but were what the prisoners had been carrying on the day they were captured. Frugal use of the precious commodity had made it last.

However, the guards were looking for soap, and this was soap. The prisoners who had some were made to kneel with a three-cornered piece of timber between their calves and buttocks. The prisoners' shoulders were forced downwards so that the weight of their body was on the timber, which the Japanese would then roll back and forth. The pain was excruciating, and prisoners who were tortured in this way had difficulty walking for a long time afterwards.

When the punishment had been meted out, the camp commandant, Sergeant Ashino, ordered the Australian officer in charge, Colonel Ramsay, to parade his men and give them a lecture on dishonourable stealing.

'One case of soap, okay; two cases, okay. Even three okay', Ashino told Ramsay. 'But SEVEN cases of soap!'

The Australian colonel, tongue in cheek, addressed the parade on the evils of thievery. While the colonel was doing this, Ashino saw a prisoner talking. He bounded from the dais and hit the man on the jaw with an open hand.

He immediately seemed sorry for what he had done. Afterwards, he sought out the man he had hit and apologised, saying he had never struck a prisoner before. 'But you must remember', he told the man, 'that when your colonel is speaking you must not talk.' He gave the man a tin of condensed milk, apparently as compensation.

Every prisoner in the camp envied the man Ashino had hit. They'd all take a whack in the mouth for a tin of condensed milk.

Sergeant Ashino was full of strange quirks. Not the least of them was his sense of humour. Asked by the camp adjutant, Captain Hence, for permission to take a work party out to cut firewood, Ashino pointed to an unoccupied house in the compound. 'Plenty firewood there', he said as he walked away.

When he returned, the Australians had torn down the house.

'What have you done?' Ashino howled. Mad with anger, he grabbed a length of timber and flailed left and right.

'We've been getting firewood', Captain Hence told him.

'Good house', Ashino yelled. 'You knock down good house for *firewood*!'

'You told us to. You said it would give us plenty of firewood.'

'It was joke.'

'Then we knocked it down as a joke.'

Ashino's anger soon subsided. He stopped hitting out with his piece of timber and seemed to see the funny side of it.

Ashino turned out to be that rare creature, a Japanese the men liked. Towards the end of October 1942, he heard them talking about the Melbourne Cup.

'Plenty cups in Tavoy. I give them, you drink.'

'The Melbourne Cup is a horse race', he was told.

'You want horse race, we have Melbourne Cup here in Tavoy.'

When it was pointed out to him that a Melbourne Cup needed horses, he said, 'Big men horses, small men ride on backs. Melbourne Cup will be important day in Tavoy, rest day for everyone.'

The promise of a rest day did it. Horses and jockeys were nominated and Ashino put up the trophies, a cup for the winning 'horse' and a whip for its rider.

An officer told him they couldn't have the Melbourne Cup without the governor-general.

Ashino was puzzled. 'What is governor-general?'

'He's the Queen's representative in Australia. Wouldn't be the Melbourne Cup without him.'

'Then one man will be governor-general', Ashino said.

'What about his carriage?'

'Governor-general has carriage?'

When told that he did, Ashino said he'd get him a Burmese yak cart.

'And what about the Melbourne Cup ball?'

Ashino grinned. 'You joking to me. You don't need ball for horse race. Ball for football.'

The Australians explained that a Melbourne Cup ball was about music and dancing.

'Ah so, music', Ashino said. 'I get Burmese orchestra.'

'And girls?'

Ashino shook his head. 'No girls. Your men the girls.'

And so it was decided. By the time the second Tuesday in November arrived, a straight strip of the compound had been cleared for the racetrack. Seating appeared from nowhere, and even grandstands sprang up.

Australian officers were appointed as clerk of the course, starter, stewards and track detectives. Before starting time, the track detectives arrested Sergeant Ashino and charged him with carrying weapons on the course and harbouring undesirables, to wit Australian prisoners of war. Sergeant Ashino's sword belt and pistol were taken from him. Everybody held their breath. Taking weapons from a Japanese meant death, but Ashino played along. He submitted to being marched to a stewards' inquiry and made to stand to attention between two escorts. The maximum sentence, a fine of one hundred Burmese cigars, was imposed.

Ashino paid up. He handed over a full carton of the best Burmese cheroots, which were passed on to those who were too sick to attend the race meeting.

Near starting time, Governor-General Sol Heffernan emerged from a hut. He wore bits and pieces of the uniforms of many nations. On the breast of his worn-out tunic were homemade medals, and his cap bore the insignia of the Imperial Nipponese Navy. He was barefooted, but so were many of the others. Cheers greeted the vice-regal carriage as it lumbered up the dusty straight, hauled by a yak. Sol waved his hand regally to acknowledge the welcome.

The bookie's ring had been busy, although no clear favourite had been installed because of doubts as to whether any of the starters had the strength to finish a hundred-yard race. The best price on offer was two-to-one, payable in cigarettes.

When the race started, skinny riders urged their equally skinny mounts onwards. Falls were plentiful. Two starters managed to get to the post, but payouts on winning bets were delayed when the protest signal went up. The second-placed rider had protested against the winner, claiming that the weights weren't right. The stewards dismissed the protest as frivolous because none of the bag-of-bones jockeys would have moved the needle on the scales much anyway, that's if anyone had actually had some scales.

Sergeant Ashino presented the trophies and announced that refreshments would be provided in the guards' mess hall. There, each prisoner was given a cup of tea and a couple of rice cakes. It was a banquet, paid for by Ashino out of his own pocket. He also bought and gave the men a large wooden chest of tea. They couldn't believe it. They hadn't had tea since their capture in Singapore.

The Melbourne Cup ball that night in the concrete school building had the music and dancing that Sergeant Ashino had promised.

The Burmese orchestra was more than a trifle off-key, but nobody noticed. The dancing 'girls', bearded and dressed in everything from grass skirts to canvas lap-laps, didn't lack partners on the dance floor until they asked the Japanese guards for a dance. The guards left in a hurry.

The best looker among the girls, none of whom would have troubled a Miss Australia contest, was Lieutenant Teddy Wheeler from Brisbane. Wheeler had a deceptive baby face that belied his rugged fighting ability. His men would have followed him to hell and back.

When Melbourne Cup day 1942 was over in Tavoy, the prisoners were quiet on their sleeping platforms that night. They felt more homesick than ever.

Not long afterwards, the Japanese army command ordered all prisoners to be moved from Tavoy to a new area. The men questioned Sergeant Ashino as to where they were going, but he had no idea. He did, however, suggest to his superiors that the men be left where they were. They liked him and he liked them, he told the Japanese brass.

In return, he received a belting for questioning an order.

After the prisoners left Tavoy, they never saw Ashino again. He was the one Japanese who had shown them compassion.

They didn't know it at the time, but ahead of them lay two and a half years of hell.

CHAPTER FIVE
NIPPON'S RULES

THE TAVOY PRISONERS were crammed into open army trucks, thirty men to a truck, with no protection from the scorching sun. It was a horror journey over rugged country. The crossing of the deep canyons was by crude bridges whose flimsy decking had two narrow wheel tracks. If a truck strayed from the tracks it would tumble into the depths.

This had 'Schoey' Schofield petrified because he had a morbid fear of heights. When they were crossing the bridges with a dizzying drop on either side, he'd sit with his army hat over his eyes. Only when someone told him they were safely across would he take the hat away.

On one bridge, they were only part-way across when Jimmy Harris, sitting opposite. said, 'Hats off, we're over.'

Schoey took the hat away. On either side of him was empty space. Terrified, he fell to the floor of the truck.

'You bastard, Harris', he moaned while Jimmy sat grinning. 'I'm not getting up until we get to where we're going.'

He was still lying on the floor when the truck rumbled to a stop and the men were ordered to get out. There were no more bridges. From there on, they'd been blown up by retreating British troops. The trucks could go no further. The prisoners had to walk.

Schoey was grateful for this, but before long he was wishing he was back in the truck. Loaded with cooking gear-the prisoners had few other possessions-they stumbled over rough roads, then along a railway line running up the west coast of Burma to Moulmein. The sharp metal on the line sliced into the feet of the prisoners, most of whom were barefooted.

Soon everyone was hobbling, but the Japanese marched them day and night, allowing only an occasional rest. Over three days and nights, they covered a hundred miles. When they reached their destination, Thambuzyat, many of them were more dead than alive.

Thambuzyat was the main workshop for the building of the Burma–Siam railway from the Burma end. It was a huge camp of about fifty bamboo and attap (palm thatch) huts.

When they arrived, the exhausted prisoners weren't allowed to rest. Work parties were ordered out to gather wood for the cooking fires, but not before the three thousand prisoners were paraded for an address by the officer in charge of the camp, Lieutenant Colonel Nagatomo.

One of the Australians, a clerk with shorthand knowledge, knew that as the railway was the start of a huge project, the Japanese officer's words could be of historic importance, so he used a stub of pencil to record the speech verbatim. Afterwards, copies were made on any scraps of paper that could be found. Bodero carried his copy throughout his entire term as a prisoner of war.

From a dais, Nagatomo spoke through a Japanese interpreter.

'It is a great pleasure to me to see you all at this place as I am chief of the war prison camp in obedience of the Imperial command issued by His Majesty the Emperor.

'The Great East Asiatic war has broken out due to the rising of the East Asiatic nations whose hearts were burnt with a desire to live and preserve their nations on account of the intrusion of the British and Americans of the past many years.

'There is therefore no other reason for Japan to drive out the anti-Asian powers of the arrogant and insolent British and Americans from East Asia in cooperation with our neighbours of China or other East Asiatic nations. It establishes the Great East Asia Co-prosperity for the benefit of all human beings to establish everlasting peace in the world.

'During the past few centuries, Nippon has made extreme endeavours and made sacrifices to become the leader of the East Asiatic nations who are mercilessly and pitifully treated by the outside forces of the American and British, and Nippon without disgracing anybody has been doing her best until now for fostering Nippon power.

'You are all only a few remaining skeletons after the invasion of East Asia and are pitiful victims. It is not your fault, but till your governments wake up from their dreams and discontinue their resistance, all of you will not be released.

'However, I shall not treat you badly for the sake of humanity as you have no fighting power at all. His Majesty the Emperor has been deeply anxious about all the war prisoners and has ordered us to enable the opening of war prisoners' camps at almost all the places in the southern countries.

'The Imperial thoughts are inestimable, the Imperial favours are infinite and those such as you should weep with gratitude at the greatness of them and should correct or mend the improper and misleading anti-Japanese ideas. I should meet with you hereafter and at the beginning of the opening of this office, I require you to observe the four following points:

'1: I heard that you complain about the insufficiency of the various items. Although there may be a lack of materials, it is difficult to meet all your requirements. Just turn your eyes towards the present condition of the world. It is entirely different from pre-war times in all countries and all materials are short and it is not easy to obtain even a small matchstick, and the present condition is such that it is not possible for needy women and children to get sufficient food.

'Needless to say, therefore, that at such inconvenient places, even our respectable Nippon Imperial Army is not able to get mosquito nets, foodstuffs, medicines and cigarettes freely and frequently. As conditions are such, how can you expect me to treat you better than the Imperial Nippon Army? I do not persecute you according to my own wish. It is not due to the expense but due to the shortness of materials at such distant places. In spite of my wishes to meet your requirements, I cannot do so with money. I shall, however, supply you if I can do so with my best efforts. I hope you will rely upon me and render your lives before me.

'2: I shall strictly manage all of you, going out and coming back, meeting with friends, communications, possessions of money etc. shall be limited. Living manners, deportments, salutation and attitude shall be strict and according to the rules of the Nippon Army because it is only possible to manage you all, who are merely rabble, by the order of military regulations. But this time I shall issue separate pamphlets of house rules and you shall not at all infringe any of them by any means.

'3: My biggest requirement from you is on escape. The rules of escape shall naturally be very severe. This rule may be quite useless and only binding to some of the prisoners, but it is most important for all of you in the management of the camp. You should, therefore, be contented accordingly. If there is a man who has at least one percent chance of escape we should make him pay the extreme penalty. If there is one foolish man trying to escape he shall see big jungles towards the east which are absolutely impossible for communications. Towards the west he shall see boundless oceans. Above all, in the many points of north and south, our Nippon army is staying and guarding you. You will easily understand the difficulty of complete escape. A few such cases of ill-omened matters which happened in Singapore shall prove the above, and you should not repeat such foolish things, although it is a last chance after great embarrassment.

'4: Hereafter I shall require all of you to work, as nobody is permitted to do nothing and eat as at present. In addition, the Imperial Nippon Army has great work to promote at the places nearly occupied by them and this is an essential and important matter at the time of such shortness of materials. Your lives are preserved by the military and you must reward them with your labour. By the hands of the Nippon army, railway work to connect Siam and Burma has started to the great interest of the world. There are deep jungles where no man comes to clear them by cutting the trees. There are also countless difficulties and sufferings, but you should be grateful to have the honour to join in this great work which was never done before and you should do your best efforts. I shall check and investigate carefully about your non-attendance and so all of you, except those who are really unable to work, shall be taken out for labour. At the same time, I shall expect all of you to work earnestly and confidently every day. You are the remnants of a rabble army and this line will be built over the bones of the white man.

'In conclusion, I say to work cheerfully and from henceforth you shall be guarded by this motto.

'These instructions have been given to you on the opening of a war prisoners' camp at Thambuzyat.'

At the end of his address, Lieutenant Colonel Nagatomo turned abruptly on his heels and strode off the parade ground. The guards dismissed the prisoners, but many stood still, stunned by what they had heard.

Peter Murphy summed up their feelings. 'What a load of bullshit', he said.

After only a few days at Thambuzyat, work parties were marched out to the part of the railway line that had been started by natives. Each work party went to a different camp.

Jim Bodero, Snowy and their mates went east to what was known as the Eight-Kilo camp. There, they found no camp, nor any buildings, only wild jungle.

The Japanese guards told them this was to be their base. They would go from here each day to work on the railway line.

'What are we going to live in?' Snowy asked a guard.

The guard shrugged. 'You build. Or you sleep in rain.'

It was raining constantly. Clothing and footwear had rotted away long ago, and the prisoners wore only what ingenuity could provide. Now they had to improvise with their shelter.

They cut down scrub and built gunyahs of bark propped against trees, just as the Australian Aborigines had done for thousands of years. However, the gunyahs provided little protection against the constant rain, and every night the men slept in several inches of water. They had nothing to lie on, only leaves and scrub. It was impossible to have cooking fires in the pouring rain, but they had little to cook anyhow.

The prisoners worked on metalling the railway line and laying sleepers. After a few days they had finished the section and were moved further up the line to what was known as the Twenty-six-Kilo camp. The Japanese knew the camps only by the distance they were from Thambuzyat.

The new camp had bamboo huts with attap roofs that were as useless as the gunyahs for keeping out the rain, which poured every day.

One advantage of the huts, however, was that instead of sleeping in water, they now had raised bamboo platforms. After a particularly heavy downpour one night, the men awoke next morning to see the rotting legs and arms of corpses sticking up stiffly out of the dirt floor under their sleeping platforms. These were the remains of natives who had lived in the huts previously and had been buried under them. The deluge during the night had caused the saturated earth to subside, uncovering their bodies.

Scabies, brought on by malnutrition and lack of vitamins, was rife. A skin infection, scabies produces constant itching and victims scratch until the infected areas-mostly around the midriff, the armpits and the crotch-become open sores.

The only treatment available at the camp was lime and sulphur. This was added to large wooden tubs of hot water that stood outside a hut that acted as a hospital. Scabies victims would squat in the tubs, immersed to the neck in the smelly liquid. It was the only way to combat the itching.

Opposite the tubs and separated from them by a barbed wire fence was a hut containing Japanese stores. One day, a prisoner who had been working for the Korean guards came back with the news that a bag of salt had been left outside the store hut.

Salt was badly needed. A substitute for sugar had been found in chindegar, the sap of the goola malacco tree, which when coagulated became a caramel the natives fed to their elephants, but there was no substitute for salt. A bagful of it lying untended outside a Japanese store hut was too tempting to overlook.

Two prisoners sneaked through the barbed wire after dark, grabbed the bag of salt and took it to the hospital hut, believing it would remain undetected there because the Japanese gave the hut a wide berth, knowing that it housed men with a variety of lethal diseases.

However, the Japanese regarded the Korean guards as expendable, so they were sent to search the hut. They didn't have to be Sherlock Holmes to know where the salt was located. It had leaked through a tear in the bag, and a white trail led directly to the hospital hut. The Koreans, with fixed bayonets, followed the trail like bloodhounds on the scent.

The prisoners saw them coming. Outside the hut, a scabies victim was up to his neck in the sulphur and lime tub. The prisoners pulled the naked man out, tossed the bag of salt into the tub , then had him get back in and sit on it. He suffered in stoic silence as the water gradually dissolved the salt, which entered his raw sores. After the guards left, the scabies victim climbed out of the tub, his skin as red as a bad case of sunburn.

Some of the salt hadn't dissolved in the tub, and because it was too precious to waste, what was left was retrieved and used by those who didn't mind the flavour of sulphur and lime.

Sickness, starvation and exhaustion continued to extract a heavy toll on the camp workforce. The Australian camp doctors told the Japanese railway engineers that with so many men affected, soon there'd be nobody left to do the work.

The Japanese, who knew they couldn't have a shortage of labour on their railway if it was to be finished on schedule, allowed the doctors to classify a given number of sick prisoners each day as 'no-duty men'. They were issued with a 'no duty' metal disc that was hung around their neck on a cord and entitled them to a day of rest.

At the end of each day's work the doctors held a sick parade and selected the no-duty quota for next day.

A British prisoner who was not sick, but exhausted from slaving on the railway line, tried to get a no-duty disc. He squinted, screwed up his eyes, rubbed at them and told the examining doctor, 'My eyesight is failing, sir. I can hardly see.'

Eye complaints weren't uncommon. Lack of vitamins was affecting the sight of many prisoners. To test how bad this case was, the doctor pointed to three shovels on a table some distance away. 'What's on that table, soldier?'

The Pom squinted and rubbed his eyes. 'Three no-duty discs, sir.'

The doctor smiled and gave him a disc.

As the railway line progressed, the prisoners had to march further to their place of work. They were guarded on the way by Koreans, who would hand them over to the Japanese engineers at the worksite.

Meals had to be brought from the camp, often over long distances, and prisoners were used for this. No guards went with them, as there was nowhere to escape to in this wilderness. The food the prisoners carried back, buckets of well-cooked rice and thick vegetable and meat stew, was for the guards. The prisoners would get a small portion of rice.

The starving men who carried back the buckets of food would be taunted by the smell and the knowledge that they'd get none of it, which was often too much to bear. Even though they'd been warned that eating any of the food would result in execution, they'd help themselves on the way back to the railway workers. To cover the reduced level in the buckets, they squatted over them. It was disgusting, but they regarded it as necessary to keep them alive and also as a way of killing Japanese. It was their form of germ warfare. Dysentery had been given to them by their captors, so it seemed fair enough to give it back to them.

Food supplies for the prisoners at the railway camps, which were always at a minimum, were being further depleted by natives and Japanese stealing them on the way up the line. The food situation deteriorated further when Dutch prisoners of war, civilians brought from Java and Sumatra to work on the railway line, used money that they had brought with them to buy rations that were meant to be used for the other prisoners.

CHAPTER SIX
FRIENDLY FIRE

DYSENTERY almost killed Bodero at the Twenty-six-Kilo camp. He was losing large quantities of blood, but was still required to work on the line every day. In the early part of May 1943, he collapsed and was taken back to the hospital at Thambuzyat.

The hospital, a couple of wooden buildings set apart from the others, had been rendered safe from bombing and strafing by Allied planes after the prisoners had dug a huge cross in the ground that could be seen from the air. However, their confidence that they'd safeguarded the hospital patients was soon to be tested.

The prisoners were allowed to spend any money they had at the hospital canteen run by an English warrant officer. Australian officers were required to pay the Japanese for board and lodging. Any money they had left was used to buy eggs and bananas for the dying.

The English warrant officer in charge of the canteen was allowed to stay in there alone at night, time he put to good use by operating a hidden wireless. He was helped each night by a prisoner who sneaked into the canteen. They knew that if they were found operating the wireless, they wouldn't have much of a future, so they invented an excuse for why they were often together; they'd pretend to be homosexual lovers. Neither was that way inclined, so they were pleased that they were never required to put their plan into operation. Meanwhile, their radio continued to provide occasional news of how the war was going.

The skies above Thambazyat were normally free of aircraft, so it was a surprise when a plane appeared at a great height one night. It approached from the west and disappeared to the east, but it was too high to be able to tell whether it was an Allied or a Japanese plane.

A quarter of an hour later, at about one o'clock in the morning, it was back. Still at a high altitude, it began circling the camp. Then it dropped two flares that lit up the hospital.

'He's going to bomb us,' somebody in the hospital yelled. 'I'm out of here.'

Those who could move dived out of their beds. Once they were outside, they looked for slit trenches, but there were none. Nobody expected a clearly-marked prisoner-of-war hospital to be bombed.

However, the plane didn't attack. After a few circuits, it flew off and the men returned to their hospital beds. Later, the sound of explosions in the distance indicated where the bombs had been dropped.

The next day, a work party was sent from the hospital to a Japanese petrol dump about five miles away in the jungle. The American bombs that were meant for the dump had missed, but only by a hundred yards or so.

Bodero was among a couple of hundred prisoners sent to shift thousands of drums of petrol from the dump. The workers, many of whom were taken from their hospital beds, were at it for twelve hours without a break until the job was completed.

In July, the Thambuzyat hospital camp had another bombing alert, this time in daylight. Four four-engined bombers flew over, travelling west to east, again too high to see whether they were Allied or Japanese planes. The planes disappeared to the east, but soon returned. Now flying considerably lower, the white stars on their wings and fuselage clearly identified them as American.

Jim Bodero and Welsh sergeant-major Taffy Eckland watched from outside one of the huts on the eastern extremity of the camp as the planes circled. When it was obvious what was going to happen, Taffy yelled to Jim, 'This time the Yank bastards are going to bomb the camp. Go for cover, boyo.'

Cover was scarce, and all they could find was a shallow drain filled with foul-smelling water outside one of the huts. They dived into it.

The bombers flew lower, now down to about a thousand feet, and continued to circle.

The Japanese guards began firing at them with their rifles. It was the only opposition they could muster because the hospital had no anti-aircraft guns.

The aircraft flew east, turned, and approached in a direct line, four abreast. As they came closer, they separated and opened their bomb-bay doors.

Lying looking up at them, Bodero saw the bombs-which he estimated to be five-hundred-pounders-leave the planes, tumble down and hit the centre of the camp, not far from the drain where he and Taffy were huddled. Timber, dirt and debris filled the air as buildings were blown apart.

The cries of the wounded stung the two men into leaving their cover and running to help. As they did, the compound erupted with more ear-splitting explosions. Fountains of earth shot skywards from delayed-action bombs that had been buried in the soil on impact and were now detonating.

An Australian officer who saw Jim and Taffy in the danger zone shouted, 'Get the hell out of there!'

As they ran, they had to hurdle a deep trench dug into the ground-the symbolic cross that everyone had imagined would keep the hospital safe from an air attack.

The four planes continued to circle the camp, and then swooped down, firing their two-inch cannons. Bullets flew around the compound and water cascaded out of holes that had appeared in the hospital's tanks.

Bodero looked for protection, but all he found to hide behind was an anthill, which wasn't much protection against bullets and bombs. Still, he crouched behind it with the childish notion that if he couldn't see the bomber pilots, they couldn't see him.

He watched a plane come in and drop smaller bombs right on the cross, so close that he was covered in earth from the explosions.

Eventually, the bombers turned and disappeared to the west.

For a few seconds, Bodero couldn't believe he'd survived. Shaking off the dirt and debris that covered him, he crawled out from behind the anthill, past a Dutch prisoner who'd had his head blown off and a dead Englishman.

Back in the hospital, he and Taffy discussed what had happened. Why would the Americans bomb a clearly marked prisoner-of-war hospital?

Jim tried to excuse them. 'They could have mistaken it for the railway workshops. They're not far away.'

'Don't tell me the bloody Yanks don't know what a red cross symbol is', Taffy snorted. 'The bastards even machine-gunned the area where the cross was.'

'They might have taken it for a gun emplacement. Or they might have been trying to stop the Japanese rifle fire.'

'Balls', Taffy growled. 'If they had enough intelligence information to know where the petrol dump was when they attacked it the other night, they must have known about the hospital camp. If they were trying to get the railway workshops, as you reckon, they must be bloody awful bombers. They didn't touch them, but they made a hell of a mess of the hospital.'

It was a terrible thing to happen. Two hundred prisoners died in the bombing, while not a single Japanese was killed, nor had the Japanese headquarters in the camp been greatly damaged.

Bodero was sent with a work party to fill the bomb craters in the road between the hospital and the workshops. Guarding the prisoners was a short, squat Japanese with a stringy ginger moustache that was waxed at the ends. The comical facial decoration was highly unusual for a Japanese.

Ginger Moustache sat holding his rifle and bayonet as he watched the prisoners work. He called Jim over. 'British number one', he said, giving him the thumbs-up.

Jim didn't argue that the attack had been American, not British. He shook his head. 'British come over … boom, boom, takusan shigoto, plenty work for POWs. British number one, no bloody way.'

'British bargoose,' Ginger Moustache said, using the Malayan word for 'good'.

Jim was suspicious now. He could see the guard was trying to get him to praise the bombing so that he'd have grounds to give him a beating. He dropped the subject.

Having two hundred prisoners killed in the bombing raid was a disaster, but the appearance of Allied bombers gave the survivors new hope that the tide of the war was turning. They figured, though, that if the hospital was going to be bombed, they might be safer somewhere else. It wasn't much of a hospital anyhow, because it had no medical supplies. The only benefits were a roof that didn't leak and work that wasn't as hard as that on the railway line.

The Australian doctor in charge of the Thambazyat hospital, Major Ted Fisher, was given a work quota by the Japanese. They ordered him to send fifty men back to work on the railway line each day. They would be replaced by fifty sick men from the railway camps, a case of sick men taking the place of sick men.

Major Fisher knew that those he was sending back to work were not fit enough, but he had no option-the quota system was forced on him.

Another doctor at the hospital, Major Hobbs, saw Fisher massaging the neck of an Australian prisoner one day and told him, 'I bet that bloke would like to be in your position, Ted.'

'Why would he like to be in my position? I've got a shit of a job,' Fisher said. 'I'm sending the poor bugger back to work on the line.'

Hobbs grinned. 'That's why he'd like to be in your position. Then he'd have his hands around *your* neck.'

Jim Bodero weighed seven stone when he was sent from the hospital at Thambuzyat back to work on the railway. The line had progressed four kilometres while he was away, and it was now the Thirty-Kilo camp.

Still weak from the dysentery that had put him in hospital, he was detailed to the kitchen fatigue party, cutting wood for the fires and carrying water. The work was heavy for sick men. Water was carried in forty-four-gallon drums cut in half and wired to a bamboo pole with a man at each end, and woodcutting involved felling tough-as-nails teak or any other timber in the jungle and carrying it back to camp in their arms.

The fatigue party had no guards, the jungle being deemed sufficient to prevent escapes. Although exhausted by the work, the men regarded it as much better than the Death Railway and its vicious guards.

The railway line had been completed to almost the Fifty-Kilo mark and small trains pulled by diesel engines were using it when one night Bodero was shaken awake by a Japanese guard. He and fifty other prisoners were to go to a nearby railway siding where they were told they were to unload a thousand sleepers.

Their hearts sank. Unloading a thousand railway sleepers would be a killer for fifty sick, undernourished men.

They were marched to the siding where a small locomotive had arrived hauling one closed wagon, far too small to hold a thousand railway sleepers.

A Japanese guard knocked a pin out of the wagon door. 'Unload sleepers', he ordered.

It turned out that the wagon held a thousand wooden clogs. It was all a matter of Japanese pronunciation-the 'sleepers' were actually 'slippers', and the work was child's play. There was a bonus, too. The wooden clogs the Japanese called 'geta' were issued to the prisoners, the first footwear they'd had since their capture.

However, when they were told that each man would be issued with a Japanese uniform, they were ready to bail up. They'd risk getting shot before they'd wear the uniform of the enemy.

Once again, however, it was a matter of Japanese interpretation. The 'uniform' turned out to be the G-string worn by Japanese soldiers. The men were prepared to accept that. At least it was something to cover the genitals.

Each man was required to sign a receipt when the G-strings were handed out to acknowledge that they had received 'one uniform complete, issued by the Japanese Imperial Army'.

Clothing wasn't all that important, anyhow; food was. They were starving. It was like winning the lottery when Bodero and Les Baird, a bushman from near Tennant Creek, were given the job of carrying a bamboo basket of hens' eggs from the railway siding back to the camp as food for the Japanese guards.

The large basket, strung between two bamboo poles resting on the men's skinny shoulders, was to be carried along a narrow path through the thick jungle. Escape was futile, so no guards were with them. The proximity of so much food without supervision was too great a temptation. They put the basket on the ground and began sucking eggs. Soon the area around them was littered with empty eggshells.

Busy sucking, they suddenly had the feeling they were being watched. Their hearts somersaulted when they realised that a Japanese lieutenant from the camp was standing watching them, hands on hips.

The sucking of eggs promptly stopped, and those that were half-sucked were carefully returned to the basket. The two men waited for the Japanese officer to draw his sidearm. They thought it was the end for them. They prepared for the worst, but there was no shot. The officer merely grinned and then disappeared into the jungle.

Hearts thumping, Jim and Les didn't stop again until they were back at the camp. They couldn't figure out why they hadn't been shot. Did the Japanese officer, not noted for leniency or compassion, feel sorry for the starving men? They'd never know, but whatever the reason, they knew they were lucky to be alive.

A few days later, a Burmese man was caught stealing food. The Japanese tied his wrists together with wire and dumped him outside the guardhouse. His flesh swelled and the wire cut deeply into his wrists. His cries of pain echoed around the camp all night, and by morning, he had disappeared.

To avoid disease, the prisoners maintained hygiene as best they could with what they had. Latrines at the Thirty-Kilo camp were open trenches. In addition, bamboo pipes were inserted into the ground all over the camp. The men urinated into these, and the urine was absorbed into the earth.

Sergeant Coombs, an Australian prisoner, was using one of the pipes one night when the Japanese camp commandant, Lieutenant Nito, saw him. Nito was roaring drunk, and for some obscure reason thought the prisoner was trying to escape, so he drew his pistol.

Coombs ran and the Japanese fired. The shot hit the Australian in the small of the back, but he managed to keep running and made it to the Australian officers' quarters.

The drunken commandant ordered the officers to hand over the wounded man, but they refused, and Nito went away.

Coombs recovered from the wound and the kempeitai held an unusual hearing into Nito's allegations that he'd shot him for trying to escape.

The trial produced one of the war's most unlikely witnesses: a Japanese guard who had seen the shooting and gave evidence for the Australian sergeant. It was sufficient for the unlikely outcome of a finding in favour of the Australian.

Lieutenant Nito was removed from the camp. Even the Japanese guards, many of whom he had beaten up, weren't sorry to see the last of him.

The death rate was high at the Thirty-Kilo camp, but the prisoners made use of the dead by burying diaries and other evidence in their graves that they hoped would be dug up after the war and incriminate the Japanese.

Jim Bodero was in a woodcutting party from the Thirty-Kilo camp when he saw another group of prisoners leading a native yak. Assuming that it was to be killed and used as meat, he told them, 'Don't forget your mates when you slice it up.'

'It's for the bloody Nips', one of the men said. 'They wouldn't give us so much as the bloody thing's roar.'

The yak's Burmese owners had followed, and when their precious work animal was tied to a tree they wrung their hands and pleaded with the Korean guard not to kill it. He laughed, aimed his captured British .303 rifle and fired. The bullet went closer to the work party than to the yak.

The Korean took another shot. This time the bullet ricocheted around the clearing. Everybody ducked for cover.

One of the prisoners had had enough. He grabbed the rifle, brought the yak down with a shot behind the ear, and handed the rifle back to the Korean guard.

'That's how you do it', the prisoner said.

Everybody held their breath. Taking a rifle from a guard was unheard of.

The Korean pulled a large jungle knife from his belt. This was it. The prisoner was dead for sure.

However, the guard confounded everyone by handing the knife to the prisoner and indicating that he was to use it to butcher the carcass.

Breathing a sigh of relief, the man cut the yak's throat, drained the blood into a bucket and sliced up the meat. This was carried back to the camp, where the Japanese conducted a quick search in case a slab of yak steak had found its way down a prisoner's laplap. Satisfied that none had, they took the meat and ignored the bucket of blood.

To hungry men, blood meant food. They left the bucket outside in the sun until the blood congealed, and then it was cut into rubbery squares that were roasted on the open fire. The men voted the yak-blood rissoles the best meal they'd had since the mouldy pie at the fall of Singapore.

Any food was memorable for men whose daily issue was a small amount of rice with an occasional pickled horse radish to provide vegetable content.

In nineteen months on the Death Railway, their only real meat came after Allied planes bombed Moulmein and killed several cavalry horses brought from Japan as officers' mounts. These were the same horses that had come to Burma on the *Toyahashi Maru*, the hellship that had transported the prisoners to work on the railway, and in whose dung they had stood for the whole of that terrible voyage.

The horses carcasses were cut up and the meat was packed into open railway wagons and sent up the line as food for the prisoners of war. It was a long journey in sweltering tropical heat to the Thirty-Kilo camp, and by the time the horse meat arrived, it was crawling with maggots.

Still, rotten meat was food. The prisoners boiled it in a forty-four-gallon drum of water, and the maggots that rose to the surface were skimmed off and thrown away, bringing partly genuine protests from some of the men that the freshest meat was being wasted.

After being cooked and eaten, the horse meat brought on more cases of dysentery.

An occasional Burmese wildfowl was the closest alternative to meat. About the size of a bantam, the birds had little flesh on them and were as tough as an old boot, but after being well-stewed in rice water, they provided some sustenance.

Bodero knew how to set spring traps. As a boy on the family property outside Rockhampton during the Depression years he'd trapped wallabies and dingoes. The wallaby skins were sold and a bounty was paid for dingo scalps. Only the skins and scalps were kept. In his current state of perpetual hunger, Jim often thought of all the meat that had been thrown away.

Now he made snares out of thread unravelled from webbing belts. The snares were set in the jungle around the Thirty-Kilo camp, close to a track used by animals at night. A sapling would be bent over and pegged into the ground, and would spring upright and catch any foraging animal that stepped into the noose.

There were no guards with the water-carrying and woodcutting details, so the snares could be set at will. Sometimes a small monkey would be caught, although many escaped because the cord made from the webbing belts wasn't strong enough to hold them.

This kind of foraging ended when the prisoners were moved from the Thirty-Kilo camp. It was the last time they were ever able to trap food.

CHAPTER SEVEN

MORE NEW CAMPS

THE new camp at the seventy-five-kilometre mark bypassed three others. The Fifty-Kilo camp was classed as a hospital camp for F-Force, while the Forty-five-Kilo and Sixty-Kilo camps were occupied by Java Force workers.

Before the men started at five in the morning, Japanese engineers measured the area to be excavated and drove in pegs to indicate the distance allocated as the work quota for the day. This had to be finished, even if it took until midnight or beyond.

Bodero, who was still weak, was put back on line construction. Though the quotas that were allotted were mostly finished by seven o'clock at night, he often worked for up to thirty-six hours at a stretch. If the quota was finished quickly, the Japanese extended it after having told the prisoners they could go back to camp when they'd completed the original distance allotted. Quick work meant extra work.

Captain Dave Thompson, the officer in charge of Bodero's excavation kumi (a section of thirty men), risked his life on a daily basis to help his men. A shire council engineer at Kyogle in northern New South Wales before the war, Thompson would follow the Japanese engineer as he pegged out the daily allocation. After the Japanese had driven in the pegs, Thompson would pull them out and replace them closer to the day's starting point, thus easing the work burden. Time after time, he risked his neck.

When the excavation was completed, other prisoners followed laying ballast, sleepers and rails, but excavation was the hardest work. The line was going through an almost impenetrable jungle of bamboo, vines, thorny shrubs, stinging nettles and other wild vegetation. Some of this country had never been trodden by human feet. The only tools the prisoners had were blunt axes, blunt crosscut saws, chunkils (a type of Burmese hoe), picks and shovels.

Wheelbarrows were unknown. When earth was removed, it was

shovelled into large bags slung between two poles and carried on the shoulders of two men, who would often have to scale tall cuttings, slipping and sliding in the mud created by the constant rain. Though each bag held between twenty and forty pounds of soil, the guards were always calling for more, more, more.

Elephants controlled by Burmese were used to carry the heavy bridge piles and girders. The elephants were almost as undernourished as the prisoners.

Constantly wet and starving, the men were developing tropical ulcers from cuts and scratches, and any wound quickly became infected. With no medical supplies, once the ulcers became established they were impossible to cure. As they spread, the only treatment the Australian medical officers could administer was to gouge at them with a sharpened spoon until the proud flesh appeared and the wound bled. There were no bandages available, so the wound would be wrapped in whatever was available, usually strips of canvas cut from tents or any scraps of cloth that could be found.

The ulcer was gouged in the hope that the germs would be expelled and new flesh would grow, but it never happened. In many cases the infection spread, and shin bones, ankles, wrists and other bones were gradually eaten away. When that happened, the infected limb had to be amputated.

Many of the amputations were performed by Australian surgeon Colonel Coates at the Fifty-Kilo camp, which had become a hospital for the F-Force men who worked on the Siam end of the line. It was a mystery why the F-Force sick were brought from Siam back to the Fifty-Kilo camp in Burma, while the A-Force sick in Burma were sent to the Thambuzyat hospital.

Before starting an amputation, Colonel Coates would ask the patient what he did in civilian life. If the man's job was one that required the use of arms or legs, Coates would say, 'We'll put this off for a little longer. In your line of work you'll need the limb.' Anyone from a more sedentary occupation would be operated on without delay. Anaesthetics were as non-existent as other medical supplies.

The patient would be placed on a crude bamboo table and Coates, who'd have a Burmese cheroot in his mouth, would thrust one between the man's teeth whether he smoked or not. The surgeon would light both cheroots and say, 'Now, lad, you puff when I puff.' Then he would start cutting and sawing. Mercifully, the patient usually passed out quickly.

Many prisoners never recovered from the amputations. Weakened by malaria, dysentery, beriberi, pelagra and scabies, they had little chance of survival.

The prisoners had no means of combating the swarms of flies that spread disease, in particular cholera, which dehydrated its victims in a few hours through vomiting and dysentery. There were no medical supplies, so those who contracted cholera knew it was a death sentence.

One night at the Seventy-five-Kilo camp, Bodero and a mate cooked rice cakes made from leftover rice they'd scrounged from the Japanese kitchen. At nine o'clock that night, they ate the rice cakes and sat talking. By midnight, Jim's mate was dead from cholera. At least it had been less painful than an amputation by Colonel Coates.

At one stage Coates was called on to finish an operation on a Japanese officer who had a burst appendix. The operation had been started by a Japanese doctor who was really a dentist. When he didn't know how to complete it, he ordered Coates to finish it for him.

'Give me back the microscope you confiscated and I'll do it', Coates told him. 'No microscope, no operation.'

'You operate or you die', the Japanese doctor said.

'Then I die. And so will your man with the burst appendix.'

The Japanese continued to threaten Coates, who continued to repeat his demands.

Finally, the Japanese gave in. Coates was given back his microscope and their officer had his appendix operation.

Coates had been an eminent surgeon in hospitals in Victoria pre-war, but he would have been completely out of place there in the overalls he wore at the Fifty-Kilo camp. He could easily have been mistaken for a workman, particularly as he often carried a brace-and-bit and handsaw that he used in his operations.

He was passing through a hut one day when a prisoner remarked, 'Here comes the carpenter with his tools.'

Coates grinned. 'The carpenter's on his way to work.'

That morning, Coates used the brace-and-bit to drill a hole in the skull of a twenty-two-year-old boy, and then sawed through his skull to expose a tumour on his brain, all without anaesthetic. By some miracle, the boy survived.

Later on during the construction of the Burma Railway, crude anaesthetics were made from herbs and jungle plants, but they weren't suitable for operations, and provided relief only as a local anaesthetic.

Operations continued to be hideously painful, and usually proved fatal.

Peter Murphy was sent to the Fifty-Kilo hospital with a badly ulcerated leg, which had to be amputated above the knee. He was recovering well when dysentery struck, and for weeks, his body, already wasted by starvation, gradually faded away until eventually he died.

Peter, the gambler who would tell people he was so unlucky that if it was raining five-pound notes he'd pick up a summons, had played his last card.

His mates buried him near the railway line that had cost him his life. Reminiscing afterwards, they said it was ironic that flies, always Peter's pet hate, were responsible for the dysentery that had contributed to his death.

Peter's fly fetish had started in Australia, on the railway platform at tiny Bororen, in Queensland. Famous for its meat pies, Bororen was a must for hungry troops going back to camp from leave. To get to the pie vendor first, Peter had hung outside the carriage and jumped before the train stopped. He'd won the race and bought out the entire stock of pies, intending to make a profit selling them to the other passengers.

First, however, he intended to have his fill. He bit into a pie and was horrified to uncover a fly. Disgusted, he tossed the pie out the carriage window. The rest of his stock followed, and Peter vowed never to eat another meat pie. It was the start of his hatred of flies.

He was in a Queensland pub swatting at a persistent one that was annoying him when the barmaid said, 'Don't you like flies?'

'I hate flies', Peter told her.

'I didn't like flies, either', she said. 'Until I opened one once.'

Peter would grin as he told the story. 'I'm so innocent it took me half an hour to figure out what she meant.'

As Peter was buried beside the railway line, his mates all had tales to tell about his notorious bad luck.

Jimmy Harris remembered the time Peter backed Morse Code in the Melbourne Cup at 10/1. Jimmy said the horse was in front with fifty yards to go when it fell. 'Pete said it was typical of his luck', Jimmy recalled.

Bodero nodded. 'Anything Peter backed found all sorts of ways to lose. We were at a dog meeting in Rockhampton and he'd backed one in the hurdle race. The only thing was, the dog had a problem. When it came to the last hurdle, it wouldn't jump, and everything would pass it.'

'Sounds like Pete, backing a hurdler that wouldn't hurdle', someone said.

'Yeah, but this one was a moral', Bodero said. 'The dog had been given a kill near the winning post and would now clear the last hurdle and keep going looking for blood.'

'Don't tell me Pete had a win for a change?'

'The dog's streets in front, it soars over the last hurdle and Peter's screaming his head off, kissing his betting slips. Then the bloody mongrel stops, lifts its leg and pisses on the hurdle.'

'Poor bloody Peter', his mates clucked sympathetically.

'Worst part', Jim said, 'he'd told a couple of the girls from a local brothel about this sure thing of his and they were very angry about doing their dough. We had to clear out before the girls got to him.'

When the laughs stopped, Sol Heffernan revived memories of what Peter had done to Dickie Barnes when they were doing their brigade training at Bathurst.

Part of the training was on sheep properties, where they were required to vault fences of wire netting topped with barbed wire. Dickie Barnes, the army's oldest soldier at sixty years of age and just about its smallest at a touch over five feet tall, had trouble hurdling the fence.

Peter volunteered to help him over. He lifted Dickie onto the fence and left him there, his legs straddling it, his backside on the barbed wire, both arms wrapped around a post like a koala. Nobody answered Dickie's calls for help.

'I reckon he'd have shot Peter that day', Bodero said. 'The bugger would do anything for a laugh.'

'Remember the wasps and Kingie the Pom?' Sol Heffernan said.

Everybody remembered what Peter did to Billy King.

The lanky Englishman had migrated before the war and become a kangaroo shooter in western Queensland, where he'd developed his skills with a rifle. When he joined the AIF, he was made a sniper.

He was with a section on patrol in Malaya in wild country between Kota Tinggi and the east coast. The only tracks through the jungle were worn by foraging animals, and bark on the tree trunks had been torn by tigers sharpening their claws. Dangerous as these predators were, the paperbark wasps were more of a hazard. Bright yellow, they were ferocious and had a vicious sting.

As the Englishman's patrol forced its way through the jungle, it disturbed a huge nest of the wasps. The men ran, but not fast enough, and the wasps inflicted a lot of pain before they were out of range.

They were sitting in a jungle clearing nursing their stings when Peter Murphy sneaked up behind sniper Billy King, jabbed him behind the ear with a pointed stick and buzzed like an angry wasp.

Kingie screamed and leapt high into the air.

When he heard the laughs and realised he'd been had, he was furious.

'He was another one who was going to shoot Peter', Sol said. 'I don't think Kingie ever forgave him.'

Now, as Peter's mates piled stones on his shallow grave beside the Burma Railway, they fell silent.

Peter, the larrikin gambler who'd kept them laughing, would be missed.

From the Seventy-Five-Kilo camp, Bodero's work party moved to the Hundred and Five-Kilo camp where the railway entered country more rugged than any they had previously encountered. Bridges had to be built over deep, fast-running streams. With little equipment, the work had to be done by hand.

In many places the railway line wound around the face of cliffs, some of which had a gradient of thirty-five degrees. Rock faces with sheer drops of a thousand feet often had to be levelled to form a bed for the line.

Timber for the bridge work was plentiful, huge teak trees with a girth of up to twenty feet and trunks as straight as a gun barrel for a hundred feet or more without a branch. Teak is one of the hardest of hardwoods, and the prisoners had to fell the towering trees with blunt axes and saws.

Piles to support the bridge decking were put in by hand using a primitive pile-driver, an iron weight suspended by a rope through a pulley mounted on scaffolding. A team of prisoners would haul the weight to the top of the scaffolding, the Japanese would call 'ichi, nee, san, shi (one, two, three, four)', and the rope would be released.

When the piles were driven and the decking was ready to be laid, girders were secured to the piles by d-spikes, pieces of iron shaped like the letter 'd' with both ends sharpened.

The decking was lashed to the girders with 'Burmese wire', a rope made from the bark of a tree that grew in abundance in Burma. When pounded, the bark became stringy. This was teased and plaited until it became a strong, durable rope.

On one bridge over a deep ravine, the piles had been driven and the girders were being laid for the decking when heavy overnight rain turned the stream below into a raging torrent. A Japanese engineer working on the bridge with the prisoners lost his footing and tumbled into the rushing water. Without hesitating, two of the Australian prisoners dived in after him.

It was a while before the two prisoners returned to the bridge alone. They'd been washed a long way downstream, they said, and were sorry but they'd been unable to save the Japanese engineer. Their rescue efforts drew high praise from the Japanese, who were amazed that prisoners would risk their lives to save an enemy.

The two Australians later confided to their mates that when they were out of sight of the Japanese on the bridge, they made sure the engineer wouldn't be coming back with them.

One day, a Lockheed Lightning twin-tailed fighter-reconnaissance aircraft buzzed the prisoners at the Hundred and Five-Kilo camp. The Allied plane flew quickly over the men, came back for a second look, and then flew off. That night, planes could be heard flying east in the direction of Siam.

At about nine o'clock, the prisoners heard a phone ring in the Korean guardhouse. The Korean voice that answered, sleepily at first, grew agitated. The men heard the word 'hikooki' (aeroplane) and took it to be a warning that bombers were on the way to attack.

The Koreans panicked, left the guardhouse and ran down the prisoners' camp lines shouting, 'Hikooki! Hikooki!'

However, it was a false alarm. There was no aerial attack, and the men decided it was probably a bombing raid down the coast. Nevertheless, the prisoners gained some satisfaction from seeing how the Koreans reacted in an emergency.

During another air raid scare one night, the Korean guards fled blindly though the Australians' lines, keen to get as far away from the railway as possible. The prisoners were delighted when one of the guards fell into a latrine trench and had to be fished out.

His smelly discomfort provided them with a happy moment.

Escape was always on everyone's mind, but there was no chance of it happening. When Japanese Colonel Nagatomo told the prisoners at Thambuzyat at the start of the Burma Railway that escape was impossible, he wasn't exaggerating.

As he said, potential escapees would see boundless oceans to the west, impenetrable jungle to the north and Japanese forces to the east and south. Prisoners whose stamina had been destroyed by slavery, starvation and disease would have no chance.

Burma had a large proportion of pro-British people, but there were also many bounty hunters ever willing to hand over escapees to the Japanese for the price on their heads.

The prisoners quickly learnt that their best chance of survival was to stay together and trust in providence.

Before A-Force arrived at Thambuzyat, a group of British POWs had tried to escape, but had all finished up in Thambuzyat cemetery.

At the Twenty-six-Kilo camp, three prisoners, Captain Mull, Sergeant Dickenson and Private Bell, had made a break for freedom, heading north towards Moulmein. All three had worked in Burma before the war and knew the area and its conditions.

Dickenson didn't last long. Badly debilitated from malaria, he gave himself up. He was taken back to Thambuzyat and executed.

Mull and Bell continued north, moving by night and hiding during the day. They evaded Japanese forces by following the Salween River but ran into a patrol of Burmese police. The escapees had no weapons, apart from an old pistol Mull had been able to obtain from somewhere. Regardless, they elected to fight.

Mull was shot dead, while Bell, who was seriously wounded, was taken back to Thambuzyat and executed.

These were the only recorded escape attempts, although prisoners caught outside a compound fence scrounging for food were also treated as escapees.

Once the men left Thambuzyat and started building the railway line, the camps weren't regarded as permanent, and no fences were erected. Without anything to stop them, the men could walk into the jungle when they weren't working, but the hostile jungle was enough to curb any desire to wander too far from the camp.

Dysentery was so widespread by the time the men reached the Hundred and Five-Kilo camp that the Japanese swabbed all the railway workers, including conscripted civilian natives, to find out how many prisoners had the disease. The swabs must have shown that thousands were riddled with dysentery, but not one person received treatment.

The swabbing was an exercise in cruelty. Prisoners were ordered to remove their trousers, if they had any, bend over and spread their legs. Then, a Japanese would insert a length of heavy-gauge galvanised wire with a hook on the end and take a sample of faeces.

Even this inhuman method couldn't destroy the Australians' ability to make fun of even the most serious situations. One prisoner pretended to join the line again for a second testing, saying he'd enjoyed it so much he wanted to back up.

The swabbing included female Burmese civilian workers. They were separated from the prisoners' compound by a high bamboo fence, but the many gaps in the fence allowed the men to witness the testing of the women.

As the men watched, one of the women gave a yell when the wire was inserted and bounded off, the wire wagging behind her like a tail.

'Told you the Nips can't aim straight', an Australian said.

The Japanese decided to make a propaganda film at the Hundred and Five-Kilo camp to show how well they were treating their prisoners of war. It was a move to counter reports of Japanese atrocities that were filtering through to the outside world.

Before filming began, the prisoners were ordered to clean up the camp. This done, tables were set up and spread with tablecloths, decorated with vases of flowers and laid out with good quality cups, saucers and plates. Fruit and cakes were heaped onto the plates. The prisoners had almost forgotten what fruit and cakes looked like.

The few who were to appear in the film were given clothes. Dressed in these, they were filmed marching out of the camp on a pretend work party. Ordered to sing a happy Australian song as they marched to show how much they were enjoying themselves, they sang *Fuck 'em All*, the camp version of *Bless 'em All*.

As soon as the film crew left, the clothes the prisoners had worn were taken back, as were the fruit and cakes.

When interpreters revealed what the happy Australian marchers had been singing, punishments were handed out and all Australian songs became suspect, so it was a surprise when the Japanese agreed to let the prisoners hold a camp concert.

One of the stage props for the performance was a wireless set, its cabinet highly polished and beautifully crafted by the prisoners. Finding the materials to make it had involved scrounging of the highest order.

The concert got under way with the disappointing announcement that star performer Bob Skelton, a talented baritone from Victoria, had been operated on for appendicitis and was in the camp hospital, unable to perform.

When it came to Skelton's scheduled spot on the program, stagehands fiddled with the knobs on the wireless cabinet. From it, softly at first, and then gradually increasing in volume, came Skelton's magnificent voice singing *Begin the Beguine*.

The audience couldn't believe it. Bob must be broadcasting from the hospital. How did the Japanese allow that?

However, Skelton wasn't in hospital. He'd left his bed to sing from a hiding place under the dummy wireless cabinet.

The illusion was incredible. No surviving member of that audience ever forgot the magical moment.

The Japanese and Korean guards were also fooled. Having a wireless was one of the more serious crimes the prisoners could commit, and the guards turned this one inside out before they finally accepted that it wasn't the real thing, only a shell.

Skelton's performance was countered by the Japanese producing a singer of their own, a senior officer who tried to outdo the Australian. In a squeaky sing-song voice, he presented a dramatic, drawn-out vocal version of ancient Japanese battles between warlords.

It was terrible, but when he wound up on a note that sounded like the factory knock-off whistle, the prisoners clapped, stamped, cheered and demanded an encore.

The Japanese officer bowed, took it as a signal of appreciation of his talent and was happy to give the audience more. Each time he finished, the prisoners called for still more. It was top entertainment seeing him making a fool of himself, bounding about the stage cutting and thrusting with his sword at make-believe foes, bellowing and grunting like a stuck pig.

'Get onto this bastard', Snowy Baker guffawed. 'The only thing not in motion is his bowels.'

When exhaustion finally brought the officer's performance to an end, he'd formed a new admiration for prisoners with such an appreciation of the arts, and treated them well for days after the concert.

CHAPTER EIGHT

TAMARKAN - AN OASIS IN A DESERT OF MISERY

SOONER or later, whatever the circumstances, the Australians would start gambling. When the inevitable game of two-up got under way at the Hundred and Five-Kilo camp, a Korean guard saw money being exchanged and pushed into the ring.

After watching the coins go up in the air and money being grabbed, he pulled a small bill out of a pocket and placed it on the ground. It was covered, the kip was tossed and the Korean lost. The winner just beat him to the money.

Scowling, the guard put a larger note on the ground. It was covered and before the coins came to rest, he'd grabbed the money and taken off. Nobody complained. He had the law on his side.

If the prisoners weren't gambling, they were scrounging something to sell. Three of them pinched a Japanese army tent and cut it into pieces to sell to the natives for sarongs. They made arrangements for the business transaction to be conducted in the jungle under cover of darkness.

One customer was a Burmese woman who wanted a sarong but had no money, so she made a physical arrangement that was readily agreed to by the sellers. Later, two of the men discovered they had syphilis. The only one to escape the disease had differing sexual preferences, and the woman had held no attraction for him.

The introduction of syphilis into the camp created a problem. There were no medical supplies to treat the many other prevalent diseases, let alone a new and exotic one.

Late 1943 was a bad period for the POWs. They were low in physical condition and morale. All contact had been lost with the outside world. The constant movement further into the jungle and uninhabited areas meant there was no news about what was happening in the war. Wirelesses that had once kept the men informed were a thing of the past, because no parts were available. Despair was everywhere. Sick men had lost the will to live.

Jim Bodero had his first attack of ulcers. Cuts and scratches that had previously healed without infection now flared into vicious skin eruptions. In desperation, he treated them with a snakebite kit he'd been able to hold on to during his imprisonment. The kit consisted of a wooden pencil-shaped phial with a lance at one end and the purplish antiseptic Condy's Crystals at the other end.

Bodero had no idea how much use a snakebite kit would be in treating ulcers. He used the lance end to cut the ulcer open, and then he'd go down to the river and let tiny fish nibble at the wound. Afterwards, he'd apply the Condy's crystals. Miraculously, it worked, and the ulcers eventually healed.

However, other men suffered badly from them, and if it wasn't ulcers, it was some other disease. Still the Japanese pushed them beyond the limit of human endurance. The Burma Railway had to be finished before the end of 1943.

And it was.

A-Force worked on the line until Christmas Day 1943. On that day at Niki, near the Three Pagoda Pass and the Burma–Siam border, they linked with F-Force, who'd been working from outside Bangkok westwards.

When the two forces met, the Burma Railway was completed.

With the line finished, the Japanese took the bulk of A-Force who were still standing-about five hundred of the original thousand men-from the Hundred and Five-Kilo camp to Tamarkan, close to the Bridge on the River Kwai of movie fame, about thirty miles from Bangkok.

For the train journey to Tamarkan, the prisoners were locked in railway wagons. On the way, they were let out to cut bamboo fuel for the railway engine when it ran out of steam. This was done many times because bamboo burns well, but not for long. Steam was both produced and lost quickly, and the train journey to Tamarkan took five days.

There, the force was split into three groups. One went to Camp Kanchanaburi and another to Non Pladuk, while the force Bodero was with stayed in Tamarkan. He didn't mind. Tamarkan was paradise compared with some of the other places where the prisoners had been kept. They were housed in sound bamboo-attap huts, and the rations improved considerably.

Food was available because Siam, although occupied by the Japanese, had not been damaged by the war. The Siamese had capitulated at the start of hostilities, and as no fighting had occurred on their soil, life for them continued much as it had before the occupation.

Farms had continued to produce crops and prisoners started to receive a small ration of greens, bean shoots and lentils. Occasionally there was even a small portion of fish and some fatty pork.

Work in Tamarkan was mainly road-building, but Bodero was put in a woodcutting party. The wood was brought into the camp by natives, and the prisoners cut it into lengths for the kitchen fires.

The men lived ten to a bay in the huts and slept on bamboo slats three feet off the ground. If they had tobacco, they could smoke until nine o'clock at night when lights-out was ordered. The blackout was imposed to foil the Allied bombers from India that passed over the camp each night on their way to bomb Saigon, the main port for the landing of Japanese supplies going by way of the Burma Railway to the Burma–India front.

This supply link was the reason for the Burma Railway. The Japanese couldn't risk transporting supplies by the Indian Ocean because by this time the Allied navies were in control there.

On moonlit nights, the bombers passing over the camp in the searchlights looked like huge white moths, and anti-aircraft guns at either end of the bridge over the river would open up. The guns didn't cause much damage to the planes, but the prisoners had to dodge flak fragments that rained down on the camp.

By this time, the bridge over the River Kwai was not the wooden structure seen in the film, but a steel bridge that had been dismantled in Java, taken to Tamarkan and re-erected.

Five of the old A-Force mates stayed together in Tamarkan-Jim Bodero, Jimmy Harris, Johnny Gorman, Sol Heffernan and Snowy Baker.

Three of the original group were missing. Peter Murphy was buried in Burma, Dickie Barnes had been left in a hospital camp and Tellemalie hadn't been seen since his open defiance of the Japanese at Tavoy, when he surely had been executed for inviting their planes to crash.

About two thousand prisoners of all nationalities were engaged at Tamarkan in road-building, ferrying supplies by river from Bangkok and various other jobs.

One huge kitchen catered for all meals. Each national group had its own cooks and cooking facilities.

Johnny Gorman, Jimmy Harris and Jim Bodero were in a work party cutting firewood for the kitchens. Also in the party was Victorian Fred Barnstable, who'd been in the Middle East with the 2/2 Pioneers and was captured by the Japanese in Java, one of the victims of the awful blunder that sacrificed returning troops when Singapore's fall was imminent.

Cutting firewood was fairly easy work and offered a bonus. Working close to the kitchen meant an occasional handout from the cooks when they needed extra firewood.

The mud-and-brick ovens produced excellent bread rolls and rice cakes. A baked dish, nasi goring, was introduced by the camp's Dutch East Indies prisoners. Made of rice, fish, onions, chillies, lentils, bean sprouts, eschalots and any other greens that were available, sprinkled with oil and baked until crisp and brown, the taste was out of this world for prisoners who for so long had existed on a minimum of tasteless rice.

Nasi goring-the Australians called it Nazi Goering-was a mile away from pap, the watery porridge made on the railway to eke out their meagre rice ration. The rice grains, after being boiled and constantly stirred, disintegrated into a gluey watery mess, somewhat like blanc mange. The Japanese had introduced pap to the men on the Burma Railway because it made the stomach feel full and satisfied. It was, however, a deceit that dissipated with the first latrine visit.

With the better diet at Tamarkan, strength gradually returned to the prisoners. However, even though they had more to eat, they couldn't resist eyeing off the Japanese commandant's private supply of hens, ducks and goats. This commandant, like those at every prisoner-of-war camp, had his own source of live food.

In charge of the commandant's livestock at Tamarkan was the Korean guard the prisoners had christened Blubber Lips in Burma. He and the other guards were the same vicious lot that had plagued the prisoners on the Death Railway.

Blubber Lips had plenty of brawn, but not much brain. Still, he was smart enough to get other people to do his dirty work for him. Each day, he'd have a couple of prisoners collect eggs, milk the goats, clean out the pens and feed and water the poultry and goats.

If Blubber Lips had had more brains, he would have figured out why there was never any shortage of volunteers for the jobs. While he lazed in the shade, the egg collectors would be sucking eggs and the goat milkers would be swallowing milk. To replace the milk that was consumed, water would be added to the pail so that Blubber Lips never noticed that any was missing. If he questioned the shortage of eggs, the men blamed the hens. When they did, Blubber Lips would grab the nearest hen by the neck and give the poor bird a sound talking-to for not working harder.

Strangely, while he took it out on the hens, he never suspected his workers.

To display their Oriental superiority, the Japanese and Korean guards at Tamarkan arranged a soccer match against the prisoners, believing that the Australians played a different football code and would have little knowledge of the round-ball game.

The prisoners recruited a couple of Brits who'd played it back home and could show them what was needed.

Finding a referee was difficult. Penalising the guards for rules infringements would be extremely dangerous. A gallant Scot, Sergeant Jock Strang from an Argyle and Sutherland unit, finally took on the job.

The game started with the prisoners bowling over the opposition using tackles that would never make the soccer manual. The Japanese and Koreans howled that this was foul play. The ref listened earnestly to their protests, knowing that while they were busy complaining, the prisoners were scoring goals. By half-time, they had a big lead, and the Japanese were slapping the ref around over his rulings.

During the break, he suggested to the prisoners that it would be safer for him, and them, if they let the guards win.

The second half saw an incredible comeback by the guards. By the final whistle, they were well in front and in a happy mood, having proven their superiority. It was important to them to be seen as superior.

This need to be superior was their reason for having the prisoners salute and bow to them. This was in evidence whenever work parties were entering or leaving the camp. The officers in charge of the workers were required to give the order 'Me ga migi (eyes right)' in Japanese as they passed the guardhouse and saluted the guards.

One big American marine sergeant from the *USS Houston* told his group, 'They ain't going to make me speak this Jap shit.' As his party passed the guardhouse, he'd salute and yell at the top of his voice, 'Take a look at those guys.' When they'd passed the Japanese, he'd yell, 'Stop looking at those guys.'

The guards, even if they knew what he yelled, took no action. He'd saluted, and that satisfied them. It was only a small moral victory, but it was enough for the Australian prisoners to start giving their own salute, a thumb to the point of the nose with fingers outstretched.

The guards accepted this time-honoured Aussie gesture as a mark of respect. They never found out that it meant something far removed from respect.

The Tamarkan guards were particularly dangerous when they were drunk. One afternoon, a party of them arrived back in camp full of sake and hell-bent on trouble. Singing at the tops of their voices, they staggered into the shed where Bodero's work party was cutting wood for the fires, grabbed the axes from them and started swinging. The prisoners quickly cleared out.

Left with nobody to hit, the guards, still waving the axes, moved on to a hut occupied by Dutch prisoners, which also emptied quickly.

The guards were too drunk to do any damage and eventually collapsed one by one. Only then were the woodcutters able to retrieve their axes.

The Tamarkan prisoners showed amazing ingenuity and skill. They restored charcoal-fuelled gas producers and used them to run refrigerators discarded by the Japanese because gas supplies were unobtainable.

With the refrigerators working again, the men had somewhere to store food for the sick in the camp hospital. The Japanese were kept in the dark about the refrigerators being brought back to life.

Now the medicines the prisoners made from the limited materials available were able to be kept under refrigeration. One of these was a yeast made from fruit peelings. The yeast had a high vitamin content and was a valuable additive to the diet of the sick.

More and more prisoners were feeling the effects of the long period of suffering, and some went mad. One young Australian, mentally deranged after a cerebral haemorrhage, threw himself down a well.

He was rescued by his mates and taken back to the camp hospital. They sat with him during the night, but when they fell asleep, he left the hospital and was crossing the bridge over the river when he was seen by a Japanese guard. Ordered to stop, he continued across the bridge, whereupon the guard bayoneted him several times. Seriously wounded but still alive, the boy was returned to the hospital where the Japanese, when they learnt he was insane, did all they could to save his life, even to the extent of obtaining blood plasma for a transfusion. However, despite their efforts to save him, the boy died.

The compassion shown to him by guards known more for their inhumane treatment was explained by a strange facet of the Japanese psyche. They respected insanity, or perhaps feared it, and would never mistreat a madman. When the prisoners learned this, there was a sudden outbreak of insanity in the camp.

Tamarkan prisoners were allowed to have cooking fires. They had lights in their huts and could smoke if they had tobacco, but not after lights out at nine o'clock.

The no-smoke-after-nine edict came about because at that time every night, Allied planes flew over the camp on their way from India to bomb Saigon and other targets, and the Japanese feared that lit cigarettes would be seen from the air.

One night, Jim Bodero and nine other prisoners who shared the twenty-foot-long sleeping platform were having a group natter when an Australian officer came in and told them it was lights out.

A guard rushed in past the officer bellowing 'Who smoke? Who smoke?'

The prisoners told him no one had been smoking.

'Nippon see smoking, Nippon see', the guard shouted. 'All men out!'

The ten prisoners were lined up outside the hut and told to number off. The guard made each man breathe into his face. When that failed to produce any smell of smoke, he sniffed their hands. Still nothing.

The prisoners really believed that none of them had been smoking. A few days later, Snowy Baker admitted that he was the guilty party. When the Australian officer had told them it was lights out, he'd squeezed the end of his cigarette and the sparks that had fallen from it through the bamboo slats to the ground had been seen by the guard, who'd been outside the hut.

The guard, when his smell-testing could find no incriminating evidence, ordered the guilty man to own up. Nobody did.

The ten men were marched to the guardhouse and lined up. The guard commander called the prisoners to attention and made them number off again. Then he said, 'Nippon guard say one man smoke. Who smoke?'

Nobody owned up.

The guard commander said, 'No man say he smoke, all men stand to attention until morning.'

Morning was ten hours away.

Fifteen minutes after the punishment began, the guard commander came out of the guardhouse and ordered the men to number off again to make sure they were all there.

Then, he selected a thick piece of timber from the woodshed. With this in his hand, he questioned the prisoners one by one.

Ray Misson, from Victoria, was first in line.

'You smoke?' the guard commander asked.

'No.' He had barely got it out before the Japanese hit him across the calves with the timber. Ray went down in a heap and stayed there.

Jim Bodero was next. 'You smoke?'

'No.' Bodero was felled by the blow, and then made the mistake of climbing to his feet. He was hit again. This time he stayed down.

Third in line was tiny Tich Hyde, from Mackay, a gnome of a man called the Mad Watchmaker because he always had a magnifying glass to his eye, tinkering with the innards of a watch. Tich was asked by the guard commander if he'd been smoking.

'No.' Tich didn't go down from the whack on the calves, but hopped about on one leg yelping like a belted dog. Even in the circumstances, it was a funny sight.

Bodero made another mistake. He laughed.

The guard commander turned on him. 'You laugh at Nippon!' He rained blows from all directions on every part of Jim's body until Jim eventually slumped to the ground unconscious. His false teeth were broken in a dozen places, his head was badly cut and his back and ribs were quickly turning black and blue.

The vicious beating seemed to appease the guard commander, and he dismissed the rest of the prisoners without further punishment.

Bodero was carried back to the hut and attended to by Dr White, the medical officer. He was unable to stand upright for eighteen days afterwards.

The guilty smoker, Snowy Baker, escaped unscathed. Snowy was embarrassed that he hadn't suffered when his mate had, but Jim told him he understood. He'd have kept silent too if he'd been Snowy.

Meanwhile, it had taught Bodero a valuable lesson. Never laugh in front of a Japanese on the rampage.

Despite the occasional bashing, the prisoners regarded Tamarkan as an oasis in a desert of misery. They had better food, less hard work and cleaner bodies after an issue of soap and permission to swim in the river. The improved conditions revived everyone's hope of survival, but the Last Post, played for those who had died, was still being heard with monotonous regularity.

The luxury of swimming in the river meant sharing it with small, sharp-toothed fish with a liking for human flesh. Nobody knew what a piranha looked like, but these had to be some kind of relation. The prisoners swam naked, and many emerged bleeding and worrying they'd been risking vital parts of their anatomy that might have some bearing on their family tree if they ever made it home.

Natives caught the fish for food. Their method was to drift along the river in a boat, splashing the water with their hands. The ferocious little fish, seeing the hands as a meal, would come up to eat. As they did, the natives would drop an unbaited hook among them. The fish, hungry enough to grab anything in sight, quickly became a meal themselves.

The river also provided another welcome diversion for the prisoners-trips to Bangkok by barge to bring back supplies. Apart from the pleasant river journey, the visit to the city meant that for the first time in all their years of imprisonment they were able to scrounge some clothing to cover their bones.

By the middle of 1944 the Allied bombers flying over the camp on nightly raids on Saigon and other east coast ports encountered no Japanese fighters or other aerial opposition and were able to roam the skies unmolested.

Japanese officers, fearing that the prisoners might try to signal the bombers in some way, sent them to the camp's outer perimeter and told them to stay there when the planes were passing overhead. They were not to look up in case the pilots saw the whites of their eyes shining in the moonlight.

The woodcutting gang was ordered to be ready to fight fires if any incendiaries were dropped. Buckets of water and bamboo poles with a rope noose at one end were placed around the camp. The Japanese told them that the noose was to be used to lasso any incendiary bombs that fell on roofs. The pole would rake down the bombs, which would be doused in the buckets of water.

They didn't explain how bombs falling from thirty thousand feet would merely sit on top of palm thatch roofs waiting to be lassoed.

The crazy firefighting methods weren't required, however, because Tamarkan wasn't bombed until after the current batch of prisoners had been sent elsewhere. It meant they never learnt whether the lasso technique was effective.

Big trees just outside the Tamarkan camp were nightly roosting places for vultures. They flew off each morning, and their return coincided with the afternoon tenko (roll call) parade. First, specks would appear high in the sky, and then the ugly birds would gradually circle lower and lower until hundreds of them settled in the trees.

As they circled the parade ground just above the men's heads, there was always some wag calling out to his mate, 'Look out, that bastard's got his eye on you.'

It wasn't all jest. The scent of death was still strong among the prisoners.

In Tamarkan, coffee-making became a thriving business for Bill, a North Queenslander. It wasn't real coffee, just scrounged rice roasted until the grains were a dark brown, almost black. With boiling water added, it was drinkable if some sweetener was available.

Bill peddled his brew around the camp calling 'Coffee Panas, hot coffee. Who wants a cup of this delightful concoction of the Orient, this Burmese liquid sunshine?'

Bill had been a beachcomber back in his native Cairns, and his sunburnt, shrunken frame was the colour of the coffee he was selling.

'Doovers', rice cakes that didn't necessarily include rice, and plug tobacco that was not necessarily tobacco, were also on sale.

The rice cakes were produced from original recipes and suspect ingredients. The plug tobacco was wild tobacco leaf smeared with chindegar sweetener and rolled tightly into a cylindrical plug. This was bound with cord and placed in the hot sun to season. Cut into thin shavings and rolled into cigarettes, the tobacco provided an acceptable smoke for those who were not too fussy.

Home brew also appeared. Stills were devised and some potent liquor came onto the market. This industry halted abruptly when, after some violent drunken brawls among the prisoners, the Australian officers ordered all stills to be destroyed.

After closing down the stills, the officers only permitted yeast to be made for medicinal purposes. Many prisoners quickly turned their hands to yeast production. They'd discovered that if enough of it was consumed, the effect was equal to that of the liquor they'd produced in the stills.

CHAPTER NINE
VOLUNTEERS - OFF TO JAPAN

IN June 1944, the Japanese command at Tamarkan issued an order. Six hundred Australian prisoners and three hundred British were to go to Japan. They would come from the main POW camps-Tamarkan, Kanchanaburi, Non Pladuk and Ban Pong.

Strangely, the Japanese called for volunteers. Jim Bodero and his mates put their hands up in the belief that nothing could be worse than what they'd been through. They were told they'd be sent to Singapore to wait for a convoy of ships to be assembled to transport them to the Land of the Rising Sun.

First stop was Kanchanaburi, where the nine hundred men were to assemble for transport by rail to Singapore. Only the fit would go to Japan, the prisoners were told. The men, all of them just skeletons, laughed at that.

The Japanese ordered a sports day to show how fit they were. There was no shortage of men who found the strength to compete when they learnt that the prize for winning was toilet paper. They hadn't seen toilet paper since 1942. Bodero, who in better days had been the hundred-yards champion of the 2/26 Battalion and Brigade, won a couple of footraces. If they'd given him a gold medal as a prize he couldn't have been more pleased.

Any sort of paper had been scarce during their time on the railway, and to enable them to roll cigarettes, the prisoners would double the quantity of any scraps of paper they came across by carefully splitting them.

In the days of the Twenty-six-Kilo camp, Padre Thorpe from *HMAS Perth* had given the prisoners pages torn from his Bible, but the men had found them unsatisfactory because they were too thin to split.

A few non-smokers who objected to the Bible being used in this way were told by the worldly padre that 'If the book is good enough to read, it's good enough to smoke.'

One race during the Kanchanaburi sports day was designed to frustrate and humiliate the prisoners. They had to run fifty yards and pick up biscuits from the ground using chopsticks. Any they picked up they could keep. However, none of the prisoners knew how to use chopsticks. When the race finished, the biscuits remained lying on the mats, tantalising the hungry men.

The Japanese thought it was funny. The prisoners didn't.

When the train left Kanchanaburi for Singapore, the men were locked in steel railway vans, fifty to a van. Packed in with no room to move, it was unbearably hot. The only air came through cracks at the top and bottom of the doors. Some men fainted, while the others fought to get their nose near one of the cracks. Those who collapsed were taken from the train and left behind when it resumed the journey. They were never seen again.

Bodero and his mates cursed themselves for being so stupid as to volunteer to leave Tamarkan.

For several hellish days, the train moved down through Malaya. When it finally reached Singapore, the weakened men expected to be returned to Changi Prison, but they were banned from there, not by the Japanese, but by other prisoners of war. The administrative staff of the Allied prisoners at Changi objected to having them there for fear they'd pass on the infectious diseases they'd brought from Burma and Siam. The Japanese apparently agreed, and they were sent to a camp on a small island about half an hour's run by landing craft from Singapore.

The prisoners didn't know the island's name, so they dubbed it Jeep Island.

Jim Bodero was in for a surprise on Jeep Island. There among the prisoners was a face he had never expected to see again. It was Tellemalie, who'd been given up for dead when he disappeared from Tavoy after encouraging Japanese planes to crash.

Years of imprisonment hadn't changed him. The cheeky grin was still there, which must have brought a few beatings from Japanese guards who couldn't be laughed at, and the wild crop of wiry black hair was as untidy as ever. Mysteriously, he hadn't lost much weight, even though all the other men had been reduced to skin and bones.

At first, Tellemalie didn't recognise the skeleton that Jim had become. When he did, he grabbed his hand. 'What are you doing here?'

'I'm on my way to pick some cherry blossoms. Nine hundred of us are going to Japan.'

'Me too', Tellemalie said. 'Should be a nice holiday.' He held out a pack of cigarettes, a brand issued only to Japanese officers. 'Have a smoke.'

Jim hadn't had a decent smoke in years. He took one, and Tellemalie lit it with a Japanese officer's lighter.

Jim took a deep draw on the cigarette.

'Good, huh?' Tellemalie grinned.

'Good all right. But Jap cigarettes, Jap lighter, fat as a pig. How the hell did you manage it, Tellemalie? We thought you'd be cactus when the Japs caught you at Tavoy waving a Dutch army hat at a Jap plane and yelling for it to crash.'

'Yeah, that was almost a mistake. I was hauled up before a young Jap lieutenant who pulls out his sword and says he's going to use it on me. I ask him why, and he tells me, "You say 'crash, you bastard, crash' to Nippon planes." Oh, that, I say. It doesn't mean what you think it does.'

Jim couldn't believe the man's cheek. 'You told him that, Tellemalie? "Crash, you bastard, crash" couldn't mean much else, could it?'

'I had to talk pretty hard to explain.' Tellemalie gave one of his lopsided grins and took a puff at his cigarette. 'I tell this Nip lieut that Australians have a strange way of speaking. When they say something, they mean the opposite. Like when a bloke's got red hair we call him Blue, and if he's fat we call him Slim.'

Jim was intrigued at the way this was going.

'I explained to him that when Australians say "bastard" it doesn't mean their mum and dad weren't hitched, it means dear honourable friend. So when I was yelling "crash, you bastard, crash", what I was really saying was "Land safely, dear honourable friend, land safely." And I was waving a Dutch army hat to show I was expressing the best wishes of all Allied prisoners of war.'

'And this Jap lieutenant believed you?'

'Not only believed me, he gave me a cup of Jap sake and asked if I'd be available to help him in his relations with the prisoners. I agreed to be a sort of public relations officer and he got me transferred to Kanchanaburi to be with him.'

'You were at Kanchanaburi? I didn't see you there.'

'You wouldn't have. I was hobnobbing in the Jap officers' mess, eating top tucker.'

'And here we were thinking you'd had your head lopped off.' Bodero was full of admiration. 'Why would you give up such a great lurk to go to Japan?'

'I started to look attractive to the Jap lieutenant, that's why. I had to get clear of him. Japan seemed far enough away to preserve my virginity.'

Bodero marvelled at the survival instinct of the man. 'You're incredible. What next?'

'Wonder if the Japs need a public relations man.'

Jim got to thinking. With survival a priority, a master at it like Tellemalie would be a good man to be around. He suggested they become a team.

'A team? You mean stick together? You and me?'

'Why not?'

Tellemalie thought for a moment. 'All right. I'll give it a go.'

Jim stayed close to his new partner when the prisoners were ordered to work on a dry dock being built on Singapore Island. It seemed a fair enough assignment, until they saw the enormous hole they were to work down. It was like an untended graveyard. There were dead and decaying bodies everywhere, with others near death lying in mud and filth, flies crawling into their mouths, eyes and ears. They were Singapore natives who for months had been working, and dying, down in that foul hole.

Fifty or more feet deep, when finished it would be big enough to hold a transport ship. Floodgates at the ocean end would allow water in, which would be pumped out after a ship entered, turning the place into a dry dock where damaged vessels could be repaired. With the Japanese shipping taking a hammering in the Pacific, the dry dock would have no shortage of work.

Prisoners hardened by years of captivity were appalled that dead and dying men were left down the hole. Even in the prison camps they'd been allowed to bury their dead.

'This is terrible, mate', Jim said.' Those bodies have been decomposing for God knows how long. That hole would have to be full of disease. We're goners for sure if we go down there.'

'Then we won't go down there.' Tellemalie was wracking his brains for a way out when, with the luck that always seemed to be with him, a solution appeared. A Japanese engineer tramped among the prisoners shouting that he wanted thirty men experienced with steam winches to work in pairs, one to drive the winch, the other to be the signalman.

The winches, used to lower skips into the hole and haul them out when filled with earth, stood on solid ground on the edge of the excavation. The winch drivers would not be going down into the hole. That was enough for Tellemalie. He held up his hand.

'You Number One steam winch driver?' the Japanese engineer asked.

'Bloody oath. Drove 'em for years at sugar mills', Tellemalie lied. He'd never even been close to one. He pointed to Jim. 'Me mate here Number One steam winch driver too. We work together.'

Bodero hissed in his ear. 'We don't know a thing about steam winches.'

'Do you want to go down that bloody hole?'

Jim shut up.

If the number of prisoners who had their hand up was any indication, Australia was a nation of steam winch drivers. Each man was asked by a Japanese officer if he was a Number One steam winch driver. They all were.

The Japanese engineer, obviously impressed by the abundance of technical knowledge of steam winches in Australia, quickly filled his quota. 'Oosh!' he said, waving them to their machines.

'Tellemalie, we're dead meat', Jim moaned when he saw the mechanical monster they were to operate. 'When the Nips find out we know bugger-all about steam winch driving, they'll shoot us for sure and throw us down in the mud with the rest of the bodies.'

The winch was a huge contraption belching steam. At the rear of the driver's cab was a steel drum around which was wound a thick wire hawser that hung over the edge of the excavation and disappeared into its depths.

Tellemalie was walking around the mysterious machinery, trying to look as if he knew something about it, when from up in the cab came a voice. 'You the relief driver?' It was a British prisoner who had been driving the winch on the night shift. The work went on twenty-four hours a day.

Tellemalie nodded dumbly, and the winch driver left his seat. 'All yours', he said. 'I've left the steam on, she's all ready to go.' Before he could be asked how the thing worked, he'd disappeared.

The two men, wondering where to start, were stirred into action by a torrent of abuse from a Japanese guard who was waving his arms around and demanding work from his new winch drivers.

Tellemalie nudged Jim forward. 'After you.'

'Why me?'

'You look like a steam winch driver.'

'Thanks, mate.' Jim climbed up and looked around for some means of controlling the thing. He yanked hard at a long lever. There was a loud whooshing sound and a string of loaded skips shot up out of the depths of the excavation. The drum behind the driver's cab whirled and screamed as it hauled in the wire rope.

Jim panicked and pushed the lever forward-hard. Just as quickly as they'd emerged from the hole, the full skips now disappeared back into it. From down below came crashing noises and frightened yells.

The Japanese guard ran at Jim and Tellemalie waving an iron bar. It was a scene that could have come from a Keystone Kops movie-two men being chased around the winch by a third waving an iron bar and yelling unintelligible abuse.

It ended when the guard couldn't catch them and threw the iron bar in frustration. It missed, and he strode off mumbling what were probably Japanese obscenities.

'I think he's pleased with us, mate', Tellemalie grinned. 'You got those bloody wagons up and back real fast. There's not much to this winch driving.'

'Then why don't you have a crack at it?'

'Me, I'm the signalman. You need someone experienced at giving signals if you're going to keep dropping wagons on the poor buggers down in the hole.'

Jim climbed back into the cab. Now that he knew which way to pull the lever, he tried it again, but not with a wild jerk this time, far more gently. The string of full skips rose out of the hole sedately.

Jim poked out his skinny chest at his success. When the skips were emptied and pushed to the edge of the pit, he applied gentle pressure to the lever and they were lowered over the side.

'What a bloody soft touch', Tellemalie said. 'I think I'll have a go.'

'I thought you were the signalman.'

'In jobs such as this, we should both be proficient.'

Jim sighed and climbed down. Tellemalie took over the controls, crouching over them like a buckjump rider waiting to be turned loose from the chute. He furthered the impression by turning up the brim of his hat, cowboy style. It was the same Dutch army straw hat he'd waved at Tavoy when he was inviting Japanese planes to crash.

It wasn't long before Tellemalie got the hang of it. From then on, he monopolised the job and became known as the cowboy winch driver.

He enjoyed himself until the day signalman Jim was standing beside a line of skips waving for them to be lowered into the pit when he pushed the lever and nothing happened. The skips didn't move.

The inaction soon had a Japanese guard jumping up and down screaming, 'Buggaroo! Buggaroo! Dame, dame!'

Tellemalie had never taken the trouble to learn any of the Japanese language, but he could see that the guard wasn't complimenting him.

'What's wrong with this bastard, Jim?' he called.

Before Jim could answer, the Jap started heaving rocks at them. It was enough for Tellemalie to desert his post and take refuge behind the winch. When he did, he saw why the skips wouldn't move. The wire rope had jumped off the drum, and coils of it were threshing about on the ground.

Tellemalie held up a hand like a traffic cop and pointed to the trouble. The guard stopped throwing rocks, the rope was put back on the drum and work began again.

However, nobody threw rocks and iron bars at Tellemalie and got away with it, so he began to engage in acts of sabotage as a means of getting his own back. He had Jim unhook the empty wagons as they were being lowered over the edge of the pit. The wagons would tumble into the hole and become a tangled pile of metal and wood at the bottom. Prisoners down in the hole waiting to fill the wagons were always warned beforehand and kept out of the way, but they played along, running about and screaming as if in mortal danger.

The guards eventually woke up to what was happening and handed out so many beatings that this form of sabotage had to be abandoned. Now Tellemalie started calling them lurid names to their faces. He figured that if he couldn't understand their language, they couldn't understand his, but soon found that he was mistaken.

The Japanese head engineer was sitting in his cane chair in the shade of an umbrella shouting instructions to the British prisoners working down below. The Brits couldn't understand a word of it. From the depths of the hole came voices calling him all the foul names they could think of.

The engineer turned to Bodero, who stood nearby, and said in perfect English, 'Those men are making it very difficult for themselves.'

From then on, Tellemalie was more careful when the engineers were around.

Queenslanders Chilla Goodchap and Ronnie Crick, sailors from *HMAS Perth*, found themselves a rare cushy job on the dry dock project. A Japanese engineer put them in charge of his personal supply of hot water.

Chilla and Ronnie had some experience with hot water. They'd swum in it when the *Perth*, along with the *USS Houston*, had been sunk in the Java battle and the sea was on fire with burning oil.

In their job as bath attendants they were required to have a huge drum of water ready at the right temperature for the engineer at the end of the day.

Chilla and Ronnie knew their job was a sinecure and, anxious to hold on to it, they never failed to have the bath ready for the engineer. He'd arrive, throw off his clothes, jump into the drum of hot water and lie back, luxuriating up to his neck.

It went on until Chilla got sick of being a bath flunky for a Jap and told his mate he was going to warm things up.

Ronnie was appalled. 'You mean boil him in his bath?'

'Course not, it'd be cruel to cook the poor bugger.'

'Then what?' Ronnie was cautious. Chilla had got him into scrapes before.

'We'll just heat his water up a bit. Let him simmer for a while.'

'He'll kill us.'

'Anyone can make a mistake. We'll apologise.'

Ronnie agreed to Chilla's scheme, as he always did.

Late that afternoon, the Japanese engineer undressed and looked appreciatively at the steam rising from his drum of hot water. He tested it with his hand to make sure it was the right temperature. 'Mizu okay ka?' he asked.

'Okay ka', Chilla replied.

The Japanese jumped in, and his mouth opened to either scream, curse or say something, but nothing came out.

'What's the problem, Ron?' Chilla called.

'I think he's trying to say the water's too hot.'

'He wants more hot water?'

'I don't think so.'

'His skin's changing colour. He seems to be shivering. We'll add a bit more.' Chilla poured another bucket of scalding water into the drum.

The Japanese leapt out of the tub, his naked Oriental body as red as a cooked crab.

The apologies didn't work, and Chilla and Ronnie went close to being executed. They were let off with a hell of a beating and sacked from their cushy job.

Chilla reckoned it was worth it, but Ronnie vowed to never again let his mate talk him into one of his madcap schemes.

When the Japanese called for electric winch drivers, Jim tried to convince Tellemalie to take on the new job.

'We're doing all right on the steam winch', Tellemalie said. 'Why change?'

'The Japs eat down at the waterfront, don't they? And where are the electric winches? Down at the waterfront. If we got ourselves posted there we might pick up a bit of stray tucker.'

Tucker? Now he was talking Tellemalie's language.

'All right, then', Tellemalie said. 'But I'm the driver, right?'

Jim sighed. 'All right, you can drive.'

When they told the Japanese they were too skilled to be kept on steam winches, they were allocated one of the electric winches. Their first sight of the complicated mass of wheels and instruments had them wishing they'd stayed where they were.

Tellemalie suddenly changed his mind about wanting to be in control and pushed Jim into the driver's seat.

'I thought you wanted to drive', Jim said.

'I do, I do. I just think you should get some experience at it.'

Jim surveyed the mass of dials and buttons. 'What do I do?'

'Pull a few levers like you did on the other bugger.'

'There's no levers. Only buttons.'

'Well, start pushing buttons.'

Jim pressed buttons and threw switches until trial and error gave him a rough idea of what worked what. In time, he was handling the winch reasonably well.

'Now you got the cow by the balls', Tellemalie told him. 'Think I'll have a go.'

Soon, both of them knew enough to get by and were able to unload cargo from the ships without causing too much damage. Occasionally, they enjoyed a bonus when ships' crews gave them some rice and dried fish. One day the handout was a glorious vegetable stew with fish and pork in it.

Other waterfront food-gatherers weren't so lucky. One lot of prisoners searching for any type of edible marine growth caught a few small crabs. They took these back to the camp and ate them, but the crabs turned out to be poisonous and two of the men died.

The men of Japan Force were never to see the dry dock finished. In August 1944, they were moved to a camp in River Valley on Singapore Island. There, watched over again by vicious Korean guards, they were ordered to build blast walls to protect the ammunition dumps.

It was hard work for Tellemalie and Jim after their soft job on the winches. Now they had to carry heavy loads of excavated earth in baskets. The guards kept count, and anyone who fell short of their quota was in for a bashing.

The irrepressible Tellemalie soon devised a method of ruining the count so that less work was involved. As the Korean guard called aloud 'one, two, three', he'd say 'six'. The Korean would continue 'seven, eight', Tellemalie would call 'ten', and the guard would pick up the count from there. It never failed. The quota of fifty bags always ended up closer to thirty.

While the counting caper was successful, it was wrong to imagine that none of the Koreans understood English. One of the guards was standing on an embankment shouting abuse in his own language when a prisoner yelled, 'Shut up, you stupid prick!'

The Korean bounded down the embankment and pushed his way among the workers. 'Who call me stupid prick?' he yelled.

When nobody owned up, everybody in the vicinity was given a bashing.

The Japanese headquarters were close to where the blast walls were being built, and the prisoners hungrily eyed a patch of sweet potatoes that were growing there. Cunning in the ways of pilfering, the Australians raided the patch many times at night without the Japanese knowing. They'd dig up the potatoes and replace the green leafy tops as if they were still growing, giving the impression that the plants hadn't been disturbed.

British prisoners, novices in thievery without leaving a trace, threw the tops on the ground, clear evidence that the potatoes were missing. The Japanese saw this and placed a guard on their potato patch.

That was bad enough, but even worse was the fact that it made them more watchful when work parties were unloading ships. Items were still being scrounged, but smuggling them back into the camp became more difficult. Anyone who was caught was in for a vicious beating, or worse.

Trading with civilians wasn't particularly productive because the population wasn't much better off than the prisoners, even though there was any amount of money. The Chinese were forging hundred-dollar bills by the thousands, but there was nothing to buy.

Once again, the prisoners who had trampled a fortune in useless money into the dust of Singapore's streets as they were being marched to Changi had access to a flood of it. Many became millionaires in counterfeit currency.

River Valley rations were drawn from the Gurkhas, well-disciplined soldiers who drilled and paraded every day to the sharp commands of their officers. These fierce Indian fighting men were sure the war would have only one result-the Japanese would be defeated. They left nobody in any doubt about the fate of any Japanese who fell into their hands.

Many were missing fingers, lopped off by the Japanese following the fall of Singapore. At first, the Japanese had tried to cajole the Gurkhas into joining them, and when that failed they were tortured. Anxious for revenge, the Gurkhas let the Australians know that arms had been hidden and they were waiting for their chance to become an underground force.

Apart from their rations, the Australians were still scrounging food, and were now able to cook it using electricity, which was a luxury they also used to light the bamboo-and-attap huts and to power homemade appliances.

Men who knew nothing about electricity made immersion heaters and other crude items that more often than not blew fuses and plunged huts into darkness.

The Pocket Battleship, a short man with a well-fed paunch, was a padre at River Valley. He was openly despised by the prisoners. Quartered with the officers at the end of a hut, he had a large wooden chest stocked with tinned food. While men about him were dying of starvation, the Pocket Battleship was eating well.

The prisoners took the edge off their loathing by resorting to humour. If a noise at the padre's end of the hut woke them during the night, somebody would comment that it was only the Pocket Battleship opening another tin of bully beef.

The Pocket Battleship's proudest possession, apart from his food supplies, was a pair of tan army officer's boots of the finest soft leather. He placed these carefully next to him each night while he slept.

One morning he slipped his feet into his boots and then quickly withdrew them again.

'Somebody shat in my boots!' the Pocket Battleship roared, adding an outburst of profanity not usually associated with a man of the cloth.

Disgusting as the act was, nobody offered him any sympathy.

Australian, British and American prisoners had another dislike-the Dutch. On the Burma Railway, they'd found them to be generally lacking in hygiene. Worse, the Dutch paid the Korean guards for rations that were intended for the other prisoners.

In River Valley, the word went out that the Dutch were buying the meat of native dogs, smuggling it into the camp and cooking it.

Medical officers had banned the eating of native dogs, fearing the animals could be diseased, and the last thing the camp needed was more disease.

When a party of Dutch men was seen carrying a covered five-gallon drum using a stick passed through the handle, six Aussies fronted them.

'What's in the drum?' they asked.

The Dutch said it was meat they had bought from the natives, and went to move off, but the Australians barred the way.

'Give us a look.' Bodero whipped the lid off the drum. It was full of water. He plunged his hand in and brought out the hind leg of a dog.

'A mangy bloody native dog!' Tellemalie snorted.

The Dutch left in a hurry. The Australians followed them into their section of the camp, where they were confronted by at least a hundred men.

Nobody knew who threw the first punch, but within seconds a free-for-all had erupted and the vastly outnumbered Australians were getting the father of a hiding.

A British work party saw the brawl and joined in on the Aussies' side. Then word spread to the Australian lines and reinforcements arrived, making the sides more or less even for the first time.

The brawl ended with the Dutch beating a hasty retreat.

The next morning, Australian medical officers taking the daily sick parade were confronted by walking wounded with black eyes, swollen faces, skinned hands, cuts and bruises.

One of the Dutch, who had a large amount of skin missing from his face, came looking for Jim Bodero. 'Did you enjoy yourself yesterday?' the man asked.

Jim recognised him as one of his personal adversaries in the brawl and was ready for the bell to ring for a second round.

'Yeah, not a bad blue', Jim said. 'What about it?'

The man held out his hand. 'It was a good fight.'

Jim shook the man's hand, and that was the end of the confrontation. It was also the end of the dog meat trade. As far as anyone knew, no more of it entered the camp.

More appropriate food became available after the Japanese arranged a fishing trip and took a few of the Australian prisoners with them. When their motorboat dropped anchor in a small bay in the harbour, the Japanese had the prisoners throw buckets of offal into the water. It wasn't long before sharks were circling. The Japanese tossed hand grenades among them and several floated to the surface belly up. The sharks weren't dead, only stunned, and it was a hazardous job getting them on board before they regained consciousness. The job was given to the prisoners.

The Japanese were so impressed when the task was completed without incident that they promised the prisoners one of the catch. Surprisingly, they kept their word and handed over a big shark. It was taken to the kitchen detail, who set about cleaning it before the Nips changed their mind.

It was like winning the lottery when they found another large fish in the shark's gut. Fresh and intact, it must have been swallowed just before the grenades ended the shark's swimming days.

The hungry men dined well that night.

CHAPTER TEN
DODGING TORPEDOES

IN October 1944, the six hundred Australian and three hundred British prisoners who had left Siam headed for Japan were paraded and told their transport convoy was ready to leave. There had been a change of plans, though. Three hundred Australians would be left at the Singapore camp and replaced by an extra three hundred British.

When it came to selecting the Australians who were to go, the Japanese took the first three hundred on parade. Among those staying behind were Tellemalie, Chilla Goodchap, Ronnie Crick, Fred Barnstable and Jim Bodero.

Barnstable, from Euchuca, Victoria, had become Bodero's close friend when they were in the same woodcutting party at Tamarkan. They were to go through some shattering experiences together.

When the convoy of Japanese ships sailed, Jimmy Harris, Johnny Gorman and Sol Heffernan were among those on board, but they never reached Japan. The convoy was intercepted by American submarines between the Philippines and Japan, and most of the Japanese ships were sunk. The American subs picked up some of the men in the water, among them Jimmy Harris, but Johnny Gorman and Sol Heffernan were never seen again.

Jimmy Harris and the other survivors were taken by the submarines to Guam and Saigon and repatriated to Australia before the end of the war.

After the first convoy for Japan left Singapore, life continued in the River Valley camp as before. It was hard yakka for the work parties, but at least they avoided the dreaded dry dock.

On 16 December 1944, the second contingent of Australians, those who'd been left in Singapore, embarked for Japan. Five hundred were taken from the River Valley camp by trucks to the docks, where they were herded onto the *Awa Maru*, a smart-looking Japanese transport ship. Also on board bound for Japan were Japanese soldiers, civilians and female camp followers.

The five hundred Australian prisoners, urged on by bayonet prods and blows from rifle butts, were forced into a hold with space for perhaps one hundred. The hold was divided from top to bottom into tiers of decks about three feet apart, into which the men were crammed. Once in there, it was impossible to stretch out or stand up.

'Like chooks in a bloody coop', Tellemalie commented as he squatted next to Jim Bodero.

When the hold was filled to overflowing with men, it was locked and battened down. The prisoners only knew they were finally under way when they heard the throbbing of the engines and felt the vibration of the turning propellers.

Hours later, the hatch covers were removed and a hundred men at a time were allowed on deck to be fed a small ration of rice. They had half an hour in the fresh air before they were herded back into their prison.

These meal breaks, if they could be called meals, were to be the only respite from the torture of the packed, stifling hold. At such times, and only then, the prisoners were allowed to use the crude lavatories set up on deck, two wooden planks that protruded from the side of the ship out over the water. They could either stand or squat on the planks while holding on to the railing, with no protection from the weather and no privacy.

The primitive lavatories would have tested even fit men, so in the prisoners' debilitated condition, and with waves slapping against their bare bottoms, drowning was a distinct possibility every time they were used.

Down in the hold, there were no lavatories, and the stench was overpowering.

The only time the men washed was when they were hosed down with salt water while on deck. Those who had tobacco were allowed to smoke in the brief time they spent out of the hold, but they had to carry some form of ashtray. The Japanese were dead scared they'd sabotage the ship by setting it on fire.

Bodero and Bill Finch, the big South Australian who'd had a run-in at Mergui with a shin-kicking Korean guard, were having one of their rare smokes when there was an angry yell and a guard came bounding down from the upper deck.

'It's the bloody Storm Trooper!' Bodero recognised the loathsome Korean guard they hadn't seen since the Burma Railway days. 'What's he going on about? You haven't done anything to upset the bastard, have you Bill?'

'Last time I saw him was on the railway', Bill said. 'It must be something I did to him back then.'

The Storm Trooper rushed at them, swinging his rifle butt, kicking and shouting, 'Burn ship! Burn ship!'

Only then did they realise that they weren't using the required ashtray.

They doused their cigarettes and the Storm Trooper went away.

As the hideous days spent in stifling agony wore on, all sense of time was lost. Daytime at least gave the men their all-too-brief spells on deck, but the nights, when they were battened down, was when the cries of sick and distressed prisoners made the blackness of the airless prison more terrifying.

The cries became screams of pure terror the night the *Awa Maru* was rocked by loud explosions. The ship shuddered violently and from above came shouting and the sound of feet stampeding on the steel deck.

Further explosions followed, and the men knew their prison was being bombed or torpedoed by their own forces. In pitch blackness, packed into the locked hold like sardines, there was no escape. If water came flooding in, they'd drown like rats.

However, no water came, and there were no more explosions. When the throb of the engines continued, the prisoners started to breathe again. The ship was still afloat and moving.

Suddenly, some sailors removed the hatch covers that confined the prisoners. The frightened men fought to get out.

Up on deck, it was daybreak, about six o'clock, and the scene was chaotic. A Japanese oil tanker that had been about four hundred yards away on the starboard side was now behind the *Awa Maru*, burning fiercely. Other ships, some on fire, were wallowing in the swell while a couple of Japanese destroyers darted anxiously back and forth. The remaining ships in the convoy were scattered far and wide.

The *Awa Maru* had been hit in the bow by a torpedo that had blown away almost the entire front of the ship. Only the watertight bulkhead had saved it and its locked-up human cargo from going to the bottom.

What was left of the convoy, helped by a cover of rain squalls and heavy snow, made for the Chinese coast at full speed to escape the attacking American submarines. There, the ships hugged the shoreline so close that the prisoners could see the mast and superstructure of sunken vessels protruding from the water. They took some comfort from the thought that the ships lying on the bottom could have been put there by the Allied bombers that had passed overhead while they were at Tamarkan.

Much later, they were to learn that soon after Japan Force left Tamarkan, the planes attacked the bridge over the river, demolishing several of its steel spans and blowing the ack-ack guns sky high.

As the Japan-bound convoy headed further north it continued to be shielded by bad weather. The prisoners had no idea where they were until one day when they were on deck they saw the clear blue sea suddenly change to a dirty brown. For miles the ship travelled through this, and then suddenly the water was blue again. They knew then that they had passed through the muddy waters that poured into the sea from the Yangtze Kiang, the Yellow River of China.

As they drew closer to Japan, the prisoners were ordered to undergo tests to determine the degree of dysentery infection among them. The Japanese wanted to assess how much of the disease they were importing to their homeland.

The men remembered the previous method of taking faeces samples using a hooked piece of wire. This time though, the Japanese used a thin glass tube. The testing was done on deck while snow was falling. The prisoners had little clothing, and shivered as they waited in line for their turn.

Nobody expected to be told the result of the tests, and they weren't. For the many who had dysentery, there was no treatment.

Jim Bodero was no longer passing blood, and seemed to have recovered from the near disastrous dysentery attack he'd suffered while working on the Burma Railway.

The *Awa Maru* and the other ships continued north and then changed course. It seemed to the confined men that they had rounded the Korean coastline and were on the last leg to Japan.

Soon they were passing through line upon line of flimsy bamboo rafts, anchored in rows a few hundred yards apart. On the bamboo deck of each raft was a huge wicker basket to hold any fish that were caught. Each raft carried a man fishing with a handline. Snow was falling, but the fishermen wore only singlets and shorts. The prisoners wondered how these men could survive the freezing nights in such skimpy clothing on rafts open to the weather. They received their answer when they saw a mother ship picking up the fishermen and their catch before nightfall.

The raft fishermen settled any doubts the prisoners may have had about the stoicism of the Japanese.

The *Awa Maru* passed other craft towing floating bundles of bamboo. Each bundle was tied to another, forming a long chain that was being brought from Korea to Japan by a method that didn't take up space on a cargo ship that was needed for more vital supplies. In Japan, the bamboo would be used for everything from building houses to irrigation pipes.

On 16 January 1945, exactly one month after the convoy left Singapore, the battered *Awa Maru* sailed into Moji harbour on the northern tip of Kyushu, one of the main islands of Japan.

As the men filed off the ship, they were watched by their sadistic Korean guards. They didn't know it at the time, but it was to be the last time they were to see them.

Haroishi was the only Korean guard for whom the prisoners had any liking. Haroishi, who made much of the fact that he was a confirmed Christian, had been with the prisoners in Singapore, throughout Burma, Siam, back to Singapore, and now in Japan. He had a good command of English, never committed any acts of hostility or viciousness and would often provide small favours. His kindnesses were such that the prisoners regarded him as a friend. They wished more of the Korean guards had found Christianity as he had.

Now, as they disembarked from the ship at Moji, Haroishi stood beside the gangway, apparently to give them a friendly farewell, but as each prisoner passed, he kicked him in the shins. The heaviest kicks were reserved for those with bandaged, ulcerated legs.

The men couldn't believe the change. Then it dawned on them that Haroishi's previous behaviour towards them in Burma was a calculated plan aimed at self-preservation. If the Allies won the war, he'd be remembered as a good Christian who had treated the prisoners well, thus making him safe from reprisals. Now that they were on Japanese soil and he wouldn't see them again, he had no need to keep up the pretence.

The prisoners added Haroishi's name to their hate list.

From the ship, they were marched to a parade ground where they were lined up and ordered to take off their clothes. It was freezing, but the tattered scraps of clothing they wore weren't keeping out much of the cold anyway.

The men stripped and stood naked in the snow that was now falling heavily.

The Japanese guards ordered them to exercise. Crowds of Japanese civilians, both men and women, stood around the parade ground laughing and jeering as the shivering, emaciated, naked prisoners waved their skinny arms and jumped about.

They were ordered to stop when the Japanese officer in charge, clad in a fur-lined greatcoat, fur gloves and a balaclava, emerged from the guardhouse and stepped up onto a wooden box. He proceeded to make a speech, telling the prisoners they were in the arms of the Emperor and should be grateful for his care and protection.

Care and protection? The icy welcome to Japan meant that many of the naked prisoners, weakened from years of maltreatment and further debilitated by the horrors of the voyage from Singapore, were to catch pneumonia and die.

When the Japanese officer stepped down from his box, the landing formalities were complete. The prisoners were broken up into groups and marched to a camp. Jim Bodero's group comprised about a hundred Australians, including old mates Fred Barnstable, Chilla Goodchap, Ron Crick and Bob Davis, and thirty Americans, marines from the *USS Houston* and soldiers of the 106th Artillery Regiment that had been captured in Java.

Flying Officer Sutherland of the RAAF was in charge of

administration and work parties in conjunction with Captain Ardsetter of the Netherlands East Indies Air Force. Medical needs were the responsibility of the Australian Army Medical Corps' Captain Higgins and Lieutenant Commander Goodman, a medical officer from the *USS Houston*.

As usual, there were no medical supplies, but the camp had well-constructed slate-tiled huts that, for a change, were dry. Each hut was divided into rooms about twelve feet square into which twelve to sixteen men were crowded. The rooms had front and back walls of glass to allow the guards to check on the prisoners.

The men slept on the floor on uncomfortable cane matting. Each man had just one blanket, even though it was the middle of winter and snow was thick on the ground. To keep warm, the prisoners huddled as close to one another as possible.

It became even colder when the Japanese issued an order that each prisoner must have his head shaved. When this was done, photographs were taken for identification purposes.

The camp was in the coalmining town of Sendryu, on the island of Kyushu, the southernmost of the main Japanese group. Nearby was the major city of Nagasaki.

The prisoners were told they were to work down the mines.

The entire population of Sendryu was controlled by the Japanese mining company. Directly or indirectly, everybody worked under the mine's administration. Rations were issued from the mine store to the town's residents on the basis of the type of work they did. No money was exchanged. Each week, the Japanese civilian workers were issued with a chit from the mine headquarters. It designated how much rice, fish, vegetables and other commodities the worker was to get.

A labourer on heavy manual work received more than someone whose job was less physical. A coalminer was allowed a bigger ration than the mine manager, a clerk or a schoolteacher. Prostitutes, considered essential for the morale and well-being of the mine workers, were high on the ration allowance list, while housewives, who were treated like a piece of household furniture, were on the bottom of the ration scale because they were not considered essential for the production of coal.

The war effort demanded that the population contribute their maximum effort. The rule was no work, no eating.

Schoolchildren were a youthful army dressed in uniforms with army ranks from one-star private up to three-star officers.

Clothing and footwear were issued to the civilians in the same way as the food rations. All the necessities were drawn by paper chit from the mine store.

One of Jim Bodero's roommates at the Sendryu camp, Ron Banks, was among those who died from pneumonia brought on by the naked exercise in the snow upon their arrival in Japan. Among the survivors in the room with him were Fred Barnstable, Mick Armstrong, Sam Atwell, Fred Asser, George Adamson, George Beavis, Frank Chattaway and Alan Campbell.

The prisoners' accommodation was based on the first letter of their surnames. Bodero's room contained men with family names commencing with the letters A to C. His identification number was jyuban (10), Barnstable's was sichiban (7) and Beavis's was hachiban (8). The three were to survive the war and remain close friends in Australia, even though they lived a long way apart, Beavis at Parklands, outside Melbourne, Barnstable at Numurkah in Victoria and Bodero at Lismore in New South Wales.

Jim had lost track of Tellemalie at Sendryu. He was in the 'M' room, M being the first letter of his assumed name, and was probably trying to talk his way out of going down the mine.

The prisoners were issued with the first real clothes they'd had in three and a half years. One set was a jacket and long pants made of a very light khaki material, a white cotton singlet and sandshoes for work in the mine. They also were given a green Japanese-style army uniform of tunic and pants to wear in the camp. Although the uniform appeared to be of good quality, it was a synthetic material made from seaweed and fell to pieces at the first washing.

All sandshoes were the same size-large. Prisoners with small feet had to flop around in footwear that was many sizes too big for them.

However, even though the size and quality weren't up to scratch, anything extra to wear was appreciated in weather that remained intensely cold.

The men, who were not required to work on their first day at the Sendryu camp, wondered about the strange structure the Japanese were building in their compound. It was a square bamboo tunnel, a yard high and a yard wide, and about fifty yards long.

When the bamboo tunnel was completed, the Japanese told the prisoners it was where they'd be trained to mine coal in confined spaces.

They had to be quick learners because the training lasted for just one day. Fifty men at a time, prodded by bayonets and blows from rifle butts, were forced into the bamboo tunnel and required to crawl on their hands and knees and take up work positions, each almost touching his neighbour in the yard-high space. The squatting men were given picks and shovels. With their pick, they had to pretend they were digging coal, while the shovel was used to throw the pretend coal back over their shoulders into a make-believe trough behind them.

Not so hard, the men thought as they played at being coalminers. They were to learn that it was a far different proposition doubled up in foul air a couple of thousand feet underground, with the only light coming from a flickering miner's lamp.

After one day of practice that was supposed to turn them into coalminers, the men were sorted into two shifts. The day shift worked from five in the morning until seven at night, when the night shift took over.

Only medical orderlies and those on kitchen duties or other camp jobs were not required to work down the mine. They were the lucky ones.

Chilla Goodchap, who'd had some medical training on *HMAS Perth*, was selected as a medical orderly, a job that separated him from his best mate Ronnie Crick for the first time. Crick joined Jim Bodero and the others as miners.

CHAPTER ELEVEN
SENDRYU CAMP

IN the last week of January 1945, the prisoners had their first taste of the real mine. They were marched to the pithead about a mile from the Sendryu camp, where they were issued with a pick, a shovel and a cloth helmet with a battery-powered lamp attached. The equipment had to be signed for, and the Japanese made it clear what would happen if any of it disappeared.

The unlucky ones drew blunt picks. A coalminer's pick looks like a kid's toy, small enough to allow it to be swung in confined spaces. The head is pointed at both ends, and if the ends are blunt, flying coal fragments can blind the miner.

When the men had received their mining gear, they were marched to the cage, the open lift that dropped them with gut-wrenching speed down the deep shaft to where a steel cable car waited. This transported them at an angle of about forty-five degrees down the main tunnel to another level. There, they left the cable car and were marched a long distance to branch tunnels where the coal was being extracted.

Coal-carrying skips ran on two rail tracks in the main tunnel. One track was used for full skips carrying the mined coal to the surface, while the other was for returning empties.

The main tunnel was roomy, and in some places, living and messing quarters were set up for Japanese miners who worked for days without seeing the surface. Many were women who carried timber used to prop up the roofs in areas where coal was being taken.

The Japanese who lived down the mine were almost white from their lack of exposure to the sun. Often exhausted, they slept, men and women together, on heaps of coal and shale piled against the tunnel wall.

Numerous branch tunnels, all about three feet high, ran from the main tunnel. Some were still being worked, while others had been mined out.

From the pithead, it took about two hours to reach the place of work. The men had to crawl the last hundred yards from the main tunnel into the coal tunnel, dragging their picks and shovels behind them.

Only the main tunnel was lit by electricity. Where the prisoners worked, the blackest of black was pierced only by the dim light of the lamps on their cloth caps. Occasionally, the lamps' batteries failed. Confined in coffin-like conditions, the feeling of being buried alive in darkness was frightening.

With little room to move, the miners swung their picks while lying or squatting between a row of posts. Between that and a second row of posts was a steel trough with an endless chain driven by an electric motor. The chain carried the coal in the trough out to the main tunnel, where it was emptied into skips.

Unlike Australian coalmines where pillars of coal are retained to support the roof, everything was taken out in this one. Two rows of ashi, thin pine posts, kept upright by pieces of pine wedged between them and the rock ceiling, were all that held the roof up. Falls were inevitable. When they came, it was a matter of luck or divine providence whether it would stop at the two lines of posts or go right to the coalface.

On two occasions, the fall didn't stop at the posts. The first time, the men managed to scamper out with their gear. The second time, they only managed to get themselves out.

Loud cracking noises like pistol shots were the only warning they had of an impending fall. Cracks speared in all directions in the rock ceiling, and the soft pine of the roof props was gradually crushed, unlike the clean snap of hardwood. When the props went, there was nothing left to hold up the roof, and down it would come.

The Japanese tried to overcome this by banning whistling in the mine. They believed that the vibrations would crack the rock ceiling and cause a fall. The prisoners didn't feel like whistling, anyhow.

As they extracted the coal, they put up a new line of posts. The trough was moved forward and the last line of posts was knocked out.

The coal seam was packed hard and tight. Using a pick while crouched almost double was as arduous as it was painful. The men found that if they dug into the base of the coalface it was easier to bring down the top coal. It was important to keep the coalface level. If a man got ahead of his neighbour, the job became more difficult. Some of the prisoners, though, couldn't adapt to the technique.

The Japanese mine supervisors continually goaded the prisoners to work harder. The only rest period was a brief meal break. They weren't allowed to leave their cramped work space, and had to eat there. They carried their food ration in their bento (lunch box), a little rice, some saccaline seed and a few pieces of pickled horse radish. Saccaline seed was indigestible, no matter how much it was boiled. The hungry prisoners ate it knowing they'd need to have the insides of a pelican to process it. The huge black pit rats had a picnic on the undigested grains.

A set quota of skips of coal had to be extracted each day. If the quota was not reached, the shift continued until it was.

The most dangerous work was at the end of the tunnel where the electric motor operating the endless conveyor chain was located. Here, the coal seam was extremely hard, and explosives often had to be used. The prisoners were required to take turns working with the sticks of gelignite and detonators that were passed man-to-man from the main tunnel. When the explosive charges were ready for firing, those nearest would be moved back a few yards.

The Japanese counted the blasts to make sure that all the gelignite had been used and none had been pilfered. Many charges failed, and a tense situation always developed when there were not enough blasts for the amount of explosives used. The guards would search the prisoners and when they came up with nothing, the men returned to the coalface. There, they worried that their next swing of the pick could hit an unexploded detonator.

Naked to the waist and streaked with sweat, Jim Bodero was painfully cramped as he squatted trying to swing his pick. Above and below him, he could hear explosions being used to bring down coal. As always, they made the foul air thick with dust and smoke. It was bad enough at any time, but now breathing was even more difficult.

Suddenly, there was a creaking in the craggy roof just above his head. He knew what it meant, but there was no escape. He held his hands over his head as the roof came down and buried him.

Fred Barnstable was the first to reach him. He dug frantically with his hands until he freed his mate. Bodero was alive, but he couldn't move. He seemed to have only cuts and scratches, but Fred knew the main injuries were internal. The Japanese couldn't see any evidence of injury, and ordered him back to work.

Bodero suffered until the end of the shift when, unable to walk, his mates dragged him along the confined space to the main tunnel. From there, he had to endure the long and painful process of getting to the surface.

Back in the camp, he was in agony, but little could be done to ease the pain.

The Australian medical officers who examined him declared him unfit for work, but were overruled by a Japanese doctor who, seeing only cuts and scratches, placed the injured man on the work list for the next day.

'I can't work, Fred', Jim told Barnstable.

'You won't be working', Fred said. 'We'll get you down the mine and then do your share.'

The next morning, Jim's mates half-carried him onto the job, and then each already overworked man did a bit extra to cover for him. They saved their badly injured mate from the Japanese brutality that was meted out to those suspected of shirking.

Going down the mine while injured had one advantage. As a worker, Jim was entitled to full rations, limited as they were. Had he been put on the sick list, the rations would have been reduced.

It was days before he could work again, and when he did start working, he hadn't fully recovered from his previous injuries when a piece of coal flew from the blunt pick he was using and hit him in the right eye. Before the shift was over, the eye was inflamed and painfully sensitive to light. It became worse in the daylight when he was finally able to come to the surface. The only relief came from keeping the eye covered.

Australian medical officer Lieutenant Goodman shook his head when he saw the eye injury. 'Sorry', he said, 'but you're going to lose the eye if it doesn't get proper treatment, and we have no medical supplies ... unless ....' He went to his near-empty cupboard. 'Unless we try this.' He held up a tube. 'It's an ointment, but it's so far out of date it's probably lost any effectiveness it had. It's certainly not an eye ointment, but we'll try it if you're willing to take the risk.'

'Let's give it a go', Bodero said. 'What have I got to lose but an eye? And I've seen enough of this place with it.'

Goodman applied the ointment, something he was to do many more times. For a week, there was no improvement, and both doctor and patient almost gave up, but then the pain stopped and the torn cornea started to heal.

'Well, what do you know', the surprised medical officer said. 'I might just patent this remedy.'

The Japanese doctor who had previously rejected Bodero's internal injuries because they weren't able to be seen put Bodero on the sick list for the eye injury because he could see this one. Amazingly, the Japanese also paid him compensation for the damaged eye. Nobody could remember any other instance of them giving a prisoner of war injury compensation. He also was given the daily food rations allocated to working men, even though he was on the sick list. The mining company also continued to pay him the miniscule daily amount the prisoners earned for hoking their coal.

'I still can't see too good', Bodero told his mate Barnstable, 'but I reckon the eye was a stroke of luck. The spell I've had off work has given my other injuries a chance to heal.'

The prisoners weren't the only ones to suffer down the mine. They often saw skips being brought to the surface carrying the corpses of Japanese. The sight of mangled enemy bodies evoked no sympathy, but it was a grim reminder of what could happen to anyone underground.

One day when the prisoners were being transported from the cage to their work, the cable car ran into a rock fall from the roof. It was brought to an abrupt halt and the men were ordered to clear the way before they started work on the coal. As they threw rocks aside, the Japanese prodded the roof with long bamboo poles, dislodging other chunks that were about to fall. It was dangerous, but the Japanese and their workers had become well-trained in dodging falling rock.

The extra work clearing the tunnel was appreciated by the prisoners. It was roomy there, they were able to work standing upright and the delay was time they would have otherwise spent crawling to the coalface for more cramped work.

'You know, Jim', Fred Barnstable said, rivulets of sweat coursing down their skinny bodies as they swung their picks, 'we shouldn't be too critical of the mine. It's snowing up top and it's warmer down here.'

'Warmer! That's the understatement of the year', Jim told him. 'If hell's any hotter I'll refuse to go there.'

Work parties marching from the camp to the mine provided daily entertainment for the local Japanese civilians. Crowds would line the roadside, enjoying the prisoners' humiliation. A few, mainly women, showed compassion. They'd grasp a marching prisoner's hand and press a few grains of corn or a couple of peanut kernels into his palm. It was a surprise to learn that not all Japanese had a hatred of the white race.

The Honeypot Ladies showed an interest in the white men's skeletal bodies. The Honeypot Ladies was the name the prisoners had bestowed on the Japanese women who emptied the contents of the deep latrine trench that ran the width of the camp. They pulled a two-wheeled cart carrying their 'honey pot', a huge wooden vat into which they'd ladle the trench's noisome contents. When the pot was full, they'd haul it out and use the contents as fertiliser on vegetable gardens.

Their arrival always seemed to coincide with the prisoners' bath time. The coal-blackened men would be in the communal brick bath, almost the size of a swimming pool, and the women would interrupt their ladling to stand giggling and gesticulating at the naked men. Sometimes a Japanese guard would give one of them a push that sent her in among the bathers. There would be much squealing and scrambling, but the Honeypot Lady was in no danger. The prisoners were in no physical shape to take advantage of her.

After their evening meal in the huge mess hall, the men were confined to their quarters. The nights, or days, depending on the shift they were working in the mine, weren't restful for the exhausted men. Electric lights flooded the glass-walled rooms at all times to enable the guards to check on numbers as they made their rounds. Fleas and bugs also prevented sleep as they feasted on the prisoners' depleted blood supply.

The fleas and bed bugs, which were enormous, would emerge from cracks in the cane matting and by morning they'd be so engorged with blood they could barely hop, and the prisoners' bodies would be covered in red, itchy bite marks.

Often, the men's sleep was further disturbed by guards shaking them awake with the trumped-up charge that they hadn't left their sandshoes in a neat row at the entrance to the room. Most times the footwear had been deliberately kicked into disarray by an earlier guard on his rounds, but the second guard, who'd be well aware of this, would mete out the snowball punishment. This involved a prisoner being made to hold a snowball in each hand as he stood to attention for hours with arms raised. If the snowball was not held tightly enough, the guard would squeeze the prisoner's hand to make sure it hurt. The torture was even more painful when it was imposed unjustly for the fictitious sandshoe breach.

The Japanese guards were all young, and had been brainwashed into believing they were a superior race with the right to humiliate lesser people. To them, the white prisoners were lesser people.

The prisoners should have been suspicious when the Japanese told them they could make a garden in the limited space of the camp. They even provided cabbage plants and pumpkin seeds. These were duly planted, and they thrived until winter arrived and the plants disappeared under a blanket of snow.

It seemed to be the end of them, but when the snow melted, the plants reappeared and warm sunshine gave them a new lease of life. In time, they became huge heads of cabbage and large pumpkins. The thought of cabbage and pumpkin soup to go with the rice and tasteless, indigestible saccaline seed was almost too much for the men.

The vegetables were ready to harvest when the Japanese confiscated the cabbages, giving the prisoners only the tough outer leaves. The pumpkins disappeared into the guards' kitchen and were never seen again.

The Japanese produced some more plants, and suggested the prisoners repeat the process. They did, but this time they made sure they beat the guards to it. The cabbages and pumpkins were only partly grown when they were harvested and eaten raw.

The garden was replanted again, but the Japanese had a guard make a daily count of the juvenile pumpkins on each vine. If one was missing, the prisoners' rations were cut for two days.

They missed the pumpkin meals, but derived a lot of pleasure from seeing a Japanese guard crawling around the garden, pencil and notebook in hand, counting pumpkins.

In another attempt to supplement their rations, the prisoners pooled any money they had and asked the Japanese if they could buy a couple of suckling pigs.

The Japanese refused at first, saying they had nothing to feed the pigs with, but agreed when it was pointed out that the animals could be fed on camp refuse that was currently being buried.

A sty was built in a corner of the compound and the guards sold the prisoners two piglets for sixteen hundred yen.

The two porkers grew quickly-too quickly. When they were big enough, the Japanese gave the prisoners their sixteen hundred yen back and took the pigs.

The men watched the squealing porkers being slaughtered and were surprised when, in a rare moment of generosity, the guards gave them the pigs' heads.

These made great soup, but the men regretted feeding them camp scraps, food they could have eaten themselves, when the result was a pork meal for the guards.

The camp commander, Lieutenant Hayashi, was a cruel and arrogant Japanese who had to be avoided when he was drunk. Anyone who happened to be in his path would be punished for no reason. He often handed over the pleasure of inflicting pain to his second-in-command, a sadist who'd flay the victim with the buckle end of his heavy leather belt, slicing out large chunks of flesh with every blow.

Equally sadistic was the camp interpreter, a runt who liked to be called Matsu-san. He had a good command of English and was notorious for stalking around the camp observing any real or imagined faults and inflicting punishment.

Matsu-san persecuted sick or injured prisoners who had been placed on the no-duty list by Captain Higgins, the senior Australian medical officer. Captain Higgins, affectionately known as Cyclops because of his large, round spectacles, was allowed to draw up this list to allow the sick and injured to rest from work that day.

Matsu-san regarded no-duty men as malingerers. He'd drag them out of their beds and make them clean grounds that were already clean, pull up weeds or carry out any other tasks he could find.

On one of the all-too-rare rest days, a camp concert was held in the mess hall. The place was packed for the performance, and guards patrolled outside.

A piano had been found somewhere and Leonard, a prisoner who'd been a jazz musician in Australia before the war, brought back plenty of musical memories.

Prisoners from all parts of the world contributed to the concert program, even the Mexicans. Two of them, from the 105th Artillery Regiment, sang unintelligible songs of their homeland.

Jim Bodero had written a verse about the obnoxious Japanese interpreter Matsu-san and, after weighing up the risk, decided to recite it.

He's stranger sure than fiction, could be one of Ripley's pars,
He's invaded our no-duties squad as Speed Gordon did to Mars.
How he came upon this earth is a matter for debate,
The date and manner of his birth is a mystery at any rate.
He shows a strain of monkey yet is of man and woman born,
You see he's partly animal and partly human form.
He's thrown our doctors, danchos, suijis and whatnot,
Even Snowy Heron's bucking mule couldn't buck this blasted twat.
He's just another mutton flap, another of that bastard race
Of slimy, crawling creatures, a reptile really out of place.
And if you should chance to meet him without a shuushin tag,
Then he'll grab you for some dirty job, the syphilitic lag.
He has more dirty crafty tricks than our RAP has pills,
He's shown more rotten lousy points than a porcupine has quills.
To see him makes one savage, burst a vessel, throw a fit.
I'd like to choke the Eastern skunk and dip his head in shit!
I hate his slant-eyed physog, this four-eyed little shark,
I'd treat him as the Sydney barber did the Man from Ironbark.
But I guarantee no tale he'd tell to any of his thieving clan,
For I'd use the sharp edge on the throat of that bastard Matsu-san.
Then no more would danchos bother us and doctors would be free
To exercise authority and give a rest to you and me.
So if by chance fate should be kind to me as one who pleads,
Then 'No Duties' need not pray for rain to stop pulling blasted weeds.

[Some words in the verse need explanation: *shuushin* is sleep, *dancho* is group leader, and *suiji* is cook. Snowy Heron, the camp *suiji*, was forever reciting Banjo Paterson poems, hence the reference to *the Sydney barber* (*The Man from Ironbark*) and *the bucking mule* (*The Man from Snowy River*).]

While Bodero was reciting his uncomplimentary verse at the concert, Matsu-san entered the hall. When the Australians saw him, they signalled frantically to Jim to stop. Blithely unaware that Matsu-san was taking it all in, he continued.

Matsu-san listened until Bodero had finished, then dragged him off to the guardhouse. The punishment wasn't as bad as Jim thought his verse warranted. He was subjected to some vicious face-slapping and made to stand to attention for a couple of hours. Bodero had expected far worse.

The rest of the prisoners, when they saw that he was still alive, said the description of Matsu-san was spot-on.

There was great excitement among the hungry prisoners when the Japanese announced that parcels from the American International Red Cross were to be issued.

The Red Cross had expected that each man would get a parcel, but when they were handed out, each parcel had to be shared by ten men, and the Japanese told the prisoners they weren't allowed to touch the contents until permission was given regarding what to eat and when to eat it. The unopened parcels, containing concentrated food, much-needed medical supplies, cigarettes, chocolate and biscuits had to be left where they were within sight and reach of the hungry men. It was additional, intentional torture. They could see them, but weren't allowed to touch them.

The outcome was predictable. Within a week, a Japanese inspection of the parcels found that they contained only empty tins and packages.

All hell broke loose. The Japanese camp commander, furious that his orders had been disobeyed, ordered that anything remaining in the parcels be confiscated. In addition, the men were to receive no rations for two days.

No rations meant that they were starved even further. The parcels that had been meant to help them in their hunger had had the opposite effect.

Still, they remembered the cabbages, pumpkins and pigs. If the Japanese guards had remained true to form, the prisoners would have had nothing from the parcels.

CHAPTER TWELVE
9 AUGUST 1945 - THE EARTH SHOOK

IN about the middle of 1945, Lieutenant Hayashi was in his cups when he let drop to Australian officers that Deutschland was finished, but Japan would fight on and never be defeated.

If Japan was invaded, he said, the Sendryu prisoners wouldn't live to see it. 'You will all be bayoneted.'

The news of Germany's capitulation flashed around the camp and raised new hope among the prisoners that the war could be nearing an end. Now the full Allied weight would be thrown against Japan. They knew that if Japan was invaded, these fanatics would die rather than surrender on their own soil. And they knew, too, that Hayashi's threat to kill the prisoners was genuine. Dead men could not report atrocities.

There was a change of guards at the camp in July 1945. Older Japanese replaced the young ones who'd hated the white man and made life hell for them. The new arrivals, past their prime and unfit for active service, brought a change in Japanese attitude towards the prisoners, both in the camp and down the mine. No longer were they beaten and tortured for minor infringements such as failing to bow or salute. The older guards went out of their way to make friendly conversation and offer help, even handing out cigarettes or some other little luxury.

Outside the camp, there were signs of growing unrest. Civilian workers watched the sky anxiously for planes, and air-raid sirens began to wail frequently, a sound that was music to the prisoners' ears.

Whenever aircraft were seen overhead, the guards asked whether they were Nippon or American. The prisoners always told them they were American B-29 bombers, whether they were or not. It never failed to trigger a Japanese rush for the air-raid shelters, huge tunnels cut into the surrounding hills.

At times, explosions from bombing raids could be heard in the distance towards the west coast of Kyushu. The war was coming closer to the mainland of Japan, giving the prisoners new heart, even if invasion meant their own deaths by Hayoshi's bayonets.

Tension mounted among the Japanese. Whenever an air-raid siren sounded, the town population took off for the hills and the guards dived into trenches dug close to the compound.

Despite the unrest, the prisoners' routine was maintained. They still went down the mine as usual.

On 9 August 1945, the men working deep underground felt the earth tremble violently. Chunks of rock from the roof above their heads broke away and crashed down.

'It's an earthquake!' somebody yelled in panic. 'The mine's caving in!'

The men huddled in their cramped space and waited for the worst, but they weren't destined to die, not then. The earth settled, the danger passed and work resumed at the coalface. It was just another incident in their ever-hazardous days, and they put it out of their minds.

However, when the shift finished and they returned to the surface, they found Japanese guards and civilians rushing about in a state of panic.

'What's happened?' Bodero asked a no-duty prisoner who'd been in camp that day.

'Nobody knows,' the man said shakily. 'Over behind those mountains to the north, towards Nagasaki, the whole bloody sky lit up in a blinding flash. There was a hell of a blast and a shock wave hit us like a tornado. Even the ground shook. How this place is still standing beats me. At first we thought it was an earthquake.'

'We felt it a mile underground', Bodero told him. 'We thought it was an earthquake too.'

The no-duty man shook his head. 'No earthquake sends up a weird cloud like that. You should have seen the bloody thing. You'd swear it was a giant mushroom. It must have swirled up into the sky for miles.

I tell you, mate, it was bloody terrifying.'

The man continued to insist that it wasn't an earthquake. 'The Japs are used to quakes, but this frightened the shit out of them. They've been running around like chooks with their heads cut off. I think they know something they won't tell us.'

'What do you reckon, Jim?' Fred asked when the man left.

Jim speculated that it could have been the oil storage tanks over near Nagasaki. 'I reckon they've been bombed and set on fire.'

'What about the blinding flash that bloke talked about? And the mushroom cloud he said rose for miles?'

Jim shrugged. 'Beats me. Could be some new high-explosive bomb the Yanks used on the tanks.'

'Some bloody bomb', Fred murmured.

That night, word raced around the camp after one of the Japanese guards let drop that the blast had indeed been a new high-explosive American weapon.

The news came in bits and pieces. It said that an atomic bomb had been dropped on Nagasaki, a bomb of such power it had completely obliterated a third of the large city and killed countless thousands of men, women and children.

Then came further news that three days earlier, a similar bomb had been dropped on Hiroshima, causing even worse devastation. Almost no one had survived.

What was an atomic bomb? The prisoners had no idea. Even when the more scientific-minded among them talked about the immense power that could be unleashed by splitting the atom, it seemed too fanciful to be real.

Anyway, they couldn't believe that the Allies would be so merciless as to use a devastating new weapon that would obliterate entire cities and populations.

It was much later that they heard of the soul-searching by President Truman before he'd agreed to use the atomic bomb. His wanted to end the war, and thus save lives, but to do so had meant killing and maiming tens of thousands of civilians.

The Allies had warned the Japanese the bombs were coming. They were told two of their major cities would be attacked with a deadly new American weapon if they didn't cease hostilities. The warnings had been ignored, but it explained the panic of the Japanese whenever they saw a plane passing over the Sendryu camp. Further, the replacement of the vicious young guards with older, kinder men could only have been an attempt to avoid possible reprisals if the war was close to an end.

Devastating as the dropping of the atom bomb on Nagasaki was for the Japanese, it didn't mean the end of work for the Sendryu prisoners. The day after it fell, they were back down the mine.

Now, however, the men had hope. Surely this horror was coming to an end. Their torture couldn't last much longer. Somewhere out in the Pacific Ocean, in the China Sea, or perhaps even closer to the mainland of Japan, friendly forces were massing.

On 15 August 1945, Bodero's shift had gone down the mine at the usual starting time of five o'clock in the morning. They worked at the coalface for five hours until a Japanese order came down the tunnel, passed from man to man: 'All men cease work.'

It was unheard of. Never before had they been ordered to stop work. It was always the opposite, always demands for more work.

The prisoners crawled out of their confined work space and sat together in the dark, wondering what it was all about.

'Could be that bomb on Nagasaki', someone speculated. 'The war might be over.'

Nobody dared hope he might be right.

The men sat in the dark for hours before another Japanese order came: 'All men out to main tunnel.'

There, they were still given no explanation as to why work had stopped. Even the Japanese mine supervisors seemed to have no idea.

Then another order came: 'All men back to camp.'

It was about one o'clock in the afternoon, six hours before the day shift was due to finish.

The prisoners returned to camp to find the men on the night shift still there. They'd been told that they wouldn't be going to work, and everyone was to assemble in the mess hall.

'I tell you, this is it', one of the prisoners said. 'The Nips are going to announce that we can go home.'

'Pigs can fly', a second man scoffed. 'I'll bet it's another of those bloody lectures they give us in the mess hall about how well they're treating us.'

One of the others said it couldn't be for one of the stupid lectures. 'They've never had us knock off work for a lecture before. And what about the night shift being told to stay in camp?'

'Could be the Emperor's birthday or something.'

Speculation continued as the prisoners were assembled in the mess hall. It was now three o'clock in the afternoon.

The Japanese camp doctor, who spoke reasonable English, climbed onto a table and held his hands up for quiet. A hush fell over the place.

'The war is over!' he said.

Strangely, there was complete silence. It was as if all the prisoners had suddenly gone stone deaf.

The Japanese doctor continued. 'Because of the terrible weapons the Americans have seen fit to use on our country and our people, Japan has capitulated and hostilities have ceased on the mainland. There is still fighting in far-flung areas, so you will remain here in camp and behave like gentlemen. Until the Allied forces arrive, the guards will remain on duty to protect you and look after your well-being.'

Only then did the prisoners snap out of their trance-like state. They shouted and cheered, hugged each other and danced. They were free, they were alive! They had beaten the odds stacked against them.

Then another reaction set in. Men cried like babies. They put their arms around their mates and wept on each other's shoulders.

The next day, only some of the aged guards remained in the camp. The commandant and his henchmen had fled.

The prisoners were now in control. With no reason to harm the vintage guards, who hadn't treated them badly, they took their rifles and sent them packing.

For men who had been cooped up for years, the euphoria of finally being free brought its own problems. Groups roamed the town looking for food. Some targeted the mine stores and took whatever was available, while others brought large jars of sake, the potent rice wine, into the camp. Deprived for so long, and with bodies left with little resistance, the prisoners drank as if there was no tomorrow. Two were to die of alcoholic poisoning.

Captain Higgins was one who let the joy of being released get the better of his judgment. He drank too much sake, and then sat naked in the huge brick bath looking out at a world of freedom through fingers pressed together in a circle to simulate field glasses.

The other three senior officers took over command and, with the help of a security detail of the fittest prisoners, gradually restored order.

Through the camp's radio transmitter, contact was made with the American forces who told the prisoners to paint 'POW' in yellow letters on the roofs of camp buildings so they could be identified from the air.

After this was done, three four-engined B29s from Guam and Saipan circled the town, dropping food and clothing in forty-four-gallon steel drums halved and welded together.

It was a fiasco. The containers were too heavy for the parachutes, and many broke free and crashed to the ground, bursting open and scattering their contents everywhere. Some drums fell in the town streets, while others crashed through the roofs of houses.

Little could be salvaged from the burst containers. Chocolates, fruit salad, biscuits and other longed-for luxuries were mixed with flea powder and disinfectants. The Americans had included the flea powder after being told the prisoners were infested with bugs. It hadn't dawned on them that putting poisonous powder in the drums together with food wasn't a wise move.

Hungry as they were, the prisoners refused the contaminated luxuries, but Japanese children scooped up handfuls of broken chocolate covered in flea powder and ate it, unaware that it could kill them.

Fortunately, ample quantities of tinned food survived the heavy landings. The hungry men ate heartily, and used any surplus to trade with Japanese civilians. Hoping to swap tinned food for fresher produce, Bodero and his mates took a supply of it out to the country farms.

They didn't know how they'd be received by ordinary Japanese, but at the first farm they came to, they were made welcome by the farmer, his wife, their seventeen-year-old daughter and her elderly grandmother. Only the wife had a good command of English, having been a nurse in a large hospital. Now in their fifties, the couple had bought the farm in better days.

When the farmer, with his wife interpreting, learnt the reason for the men's visit, he readily agreed to swap his fresh produce for the tinned variety. When the transaction was completed, he insisted that the men stay and eat with them. The food, supplemented by cherry wine and carrot brandy, was an unbelievable treat for men who couldn't remember the last time they'd had a home-cooked meal.

They ate Japanese-style seated on cushions around a low table. The women didn't sit with them, but stood close by, ready to attend to their every need. The English-speaking wife told them it was traditional in Japan for women to do this; the man was the undisputed head of the household.

The surprised Australians said the women in their country had equal status with men.

Equally surprised, she told them that women in Japan did heavy work in the fields, often behind an ox-pulled plough. 'If some farms do not have an ox, the woman pulls the plough.'

When the men said an Australian woman could please herself whether she helped her husband, the wife interpreted for her husband. The farmer shook his head in dismay and mumbled something in his own language.

'What did papa-san say?' Bodero asked.

'He say no wonder Nippon went close to winning the war.'

Everybody laughed. It was an enjoyable afternoon, almost like being back home. The friendliness was genuine, almost overpowering.

Much of Jim Bodero's hatred of the Japanese dissipated that day. This family made him realise that the blame for the war rested not with the Japanese people, but with the militarist ambitions of their warlords.

During the afternoon, the family album was produced. As the wife turned the pages, she quickly skimmed over a photograph of a young naval officer in his twenties in full Japanese uniform.

Jim turned back to it and asked who it was.

Tears rolled down the woman's cheeks. Sobbing, she told him the photograph was of their only son, who had lost his life in a naval battle somewhere in the Pacific. She wept, she said, not because of the loss of a son, but because of shame that one of the family had been killing other human beings in the war. She had tried to hide the picture because showing it to those her son had been fighting would add to the shame.

Jim Bodero found himself weeping with her. He never forgot her tears, nor her hatred of war. It did much to help him forgive those who had treated him so badly.

When they embraced and wept together in that Japanese house, he had never felt so homesick for those he'd left behind in Australia. The woman had treated him as if he was the son she had lost, while far from home, it was as if he had found the mother he had left behind.

The Australians left the Japanese farm that day with changed views, spiritually enriched and enlightened.

With time on their hands and able to do whatever they wanted, it was inevitable that the freed POWs would get up to some mischief. A group of them, led by none other than Tellemalie, confiscated a steam locomotive from a rail depot.

'I'll drive', Tellemalie said. 'I've had experience as a steam driver.'

Bewildered by the array of instruments, he had no idea how to start the thing. One of the men with him had worked for the railway back home, so he took over, and with him at the controls, the loco was driven out of the depot with former prisoners of war hanging off it. They had no idea where they were heading, no knowledge of Japanese railway signals and no thought that other traffic might be on the line.

On the open track, it was full steam ahead. With yahooing Australians perched everywhere, the loco shot through sidings and stations in a cloud of smoke, leaving female signal operators gaping in astonishment.

It was a miracle that there was no other traffic on the line. Only when a party of civilian police officers risked life and limb by standing in the centre of the railway track did they bring the loco to a hissing halt.

Japanese police! Now the men were for it.

However, instead of throwing them all into a cell, the police drove them back to camp and asked them not to do it again.

How times had changed! Not so long ago, on another railway, the Japanese would have executed them for not bowing to them, let alone stealing a locomotive.

Another group foraging around the town found a huge godown, a Japanese warehouse, packed floor-to-ceiling with thousands of American International Red Cross parcels, mostly unopened. Those that had been broached were missing only cigarettes. Now it became clear where the Japanese guards had been getting the American brands they smoked.

Cigarettes, had they been issued to the prisoners they were meant for, wouldn't have saved any lives, but the food that had been left in the parcels, a whole warehouse full of it, certainly would have if it had been issued to the starving men as the Red Cross intended, one parcel per man each month.

In three and a half years, the prisoners had received only one issue of parcels, one parcel for every ten men, and even then they had had to steal the contents.

Their captors' reason for stockpiling the relief parcels was typical Japanese logic. A Red Cross parcel a month to each man would have resulted in less debilitated bodies. Starving and exhausted, they weren't likely to try to escape like the well-fed Japanese POWs in Australia had at Cowra. Men who were weak from starvation posed no threat.

It was this kind of thinking that ruined Red Cross efforts to relieve the suffering.

Changed Japanese attitudes became apparent when Bodero, Barnstable and a few of their mates were allowed into the town movie cinema free of charge. However, after sitting through a long and boring film with unintelligible dialogue, they couldn't imagine anyone paying to get in.

By the time the film finished, night had fallen. The men were on their way back to camp when they came upon a red-light district. They knocked on a door, a flap opened and a girl's face appeared. Despite language difficulties, they were able to establish that the house worked only by day and slept by night.

'What a lousy bloody union you must have', Barnstable told the girl.

She still wouldn't let them in, even when they said they only wanted to look at the place, not use it. An argument developed, and the noise was sufficient to draw the attention of a Japanese policeman, who provided another example of the changed Japanese attitudes. Instead of running the men in, he gently advised them that it would be better if they moved on.

He left, but they didn't. Barnstable suggested going round to the back of the house to see if there was an entrance there. It was pitch dark now, and he led the single file of men that groped its way along a narrow path around the building.

Suddenly, Barnstable disappeared. The others heard a splash, and then his voice came from a long way off. 'Get me out of here!'

The men could see nothing, and felt their way along the path, which led to a well. Stumbling along in the dark, Fred hadn't realised that the path led to a well, and he was now splashing about in it. Luckily, the well was fairly full, and his mates were able to reach down and fish him out. Fred was nearly frozen by the time they got back to camp, and his mates were kept busy pulling leeches off his shivering body.

CHAPTER THIRTEEN
SURRENDER

ON 22 August 1945, a message was posted at Sendryu camp under the signature of the Commander of the Fukuoka POW Camps. Jim Bodero kept a copy of it.

I am pleased to inform you that we were instructed by the military authorities that hostilities ceased on August 18.

During your long stay in Japan as P.W. you must, I fear, have suffered and endured many hardships. Having survived these difficult times, however, your dreams of repatriation are soon to be realised.

Your hearts must be full of joy at the thoughts of meeting your loved ones, parents, wives, children and friends. I offer you my sincere congratulations and at the same time express my regret for those who have passed away as a result of disease or some other unfortunate mischance without ever having the chance and joy of greeting this happy day.

Obeying instructions, the camp staffs and I have done all in our power to help and protect you, but owing to the difficult internal war conditions we regret that we were not able to do half as much as we wished. Nevertheless I trust that you will understand the predicament in which we found ourselves.

Several days ago at one camp the prisoners presented the camp staff and factory foreman with part of their valuable relief foodstuffs and personal belongings, while at other camps prisoners have asked for permission to help civilian sufferers with their personal belongings. This is an example of your generous and understanding spirit and gentlemanliness.

For all this we, the camp staffs and I, express our deepest gratitude. Until you are transferred to Allied hands at a port that will be designated later, you must wait at your respective camps. Therefore I sincerely hope that you will wait quietly, taking care of your health, and still obeying the rules of your camps as before, thus maintaining the honour and dignity of your great nations.

About a month after the Japanese surrender, word was received that the Americans were ready to evacuate the prisoners.

The men boarded trains at Sendryu railway station and travelled to Nagasaki through country that showed signs of the air raids that had preceded the dropping of the atom bomb.

Passing through one town, they were puzzled by the burnt-out aircraft lying in the streets. A closer look revealed that it was not a town, but an aerodrome made to look like a town. The 'streets' were actually runways disguised by houses lining each side of them. The subterfuge had not deceived the Allied pilots, however, and the place had been thoroughly bombed, destroying the fighter planes on the ground.

When the men reached Nagasaki, they were aghast at the devastation, mile after mile of it. All that was left of the city were the shattered remains of a few concrete buildings. Vast areas were flattened, burnt and blackened. As far as the eye could see, which was to the tops of the surrounding hills, no vegetation remained. Charred tree stumps were the only indication of any greenery ever having grown there.

The huge shipbuilding yards on the waterfront were a mass of twisted steel. Molten metal had run down the pylons and congealed like melted wax on candles.

The railway tracks the men were travelling on were the only thing that was undamaged, having been re-laid after the bombing.

Hundreds of Japanese men, women and children wandered aimlessly among the ruins, their faces still masks of terror. Strips of skin and flesh hung from their burnt bodies.

The released prisoners, on their way home to a land almost untouched by war, were sad for these devastated people. They wondered whether their own lives were worth what had happened in Nagasaki and Hiroshima.

It was tragic to learn that it needn't have happened. If Emperor Hirohito had rejected the demands of the warlords to continue fighting, the atom bomb would never have been dropped.

After leaving the train at Nagasaki, the men were moved to an area set aside for decontamination and medical treatment.

Here, they were looked after by American nurses, the first white women the repatriates had seen in three and a half years. In their presence, the men were shy and uncomfortable about their physical appearance. No longer were they the fabled big, bronzed Anzacs from Down Under. Now, they were pitiful skeletons.

After the medical procedures were completed, the injured and sick were moved to a hospital ship anchored in the harbour. Those who were able to walk were taken to an American aircraft carrier, the *USS Chenango*, which had just come from the war zone and bore the scars of battle. Holes in the carrier's superstructure and other damage showed where a kamikaze pilot had crashed his death plane.

With the repatriated men, including Bodero and several of his mates, now on board, the *Chenango* set off at full speed for Okinawa, south of Japan. On deck, the men were lapping up their new life of luxury when suddenly sirens sounded, orders were shouted and the carrier's crew ran about urgently.

'Just our bloody luck to get sunk by a torpedo when the war's over and we're on our way home', someone said. Everybody scanned the sea, anxiously looking for the telltale white trail.

'Forget the sirens, guys', an American sailor grinned. 'We're just changing course to miss the goddam typhoon that's right in our path.'

The repatriates started breathing again.

The carrier changed course and increased speed, heading west towards the Chinese mainland. Later, the typhoon avoided, the *Chenango* resumed its original course for Okinawa. A few hours later, it entered the port of Naha.

The typhoon had devastated Naha, and hardly anything had been left intact. Ships had capsized in the harbour, and planes had been wrecked at the airfield. Had the typhoon arrived before the war ended so dramatically, it would have set back plans for the invasion of Japan because the Allied fleet had been anchored in Naha harbour.

The repatriates were housed in temporary quarters on Okinawa under American command. There was no discrimination according to rank. Privates, dixies in hand, lined up for meals with major-generals and brigadiers.

The stay on the island, which was short and sweet, came to an end when the repatriated prisoners were flown to Manila. On landing at Clark Airfield, they were taken to a large camp and accommodated in tents to await the next stage of their journey home.

Men of various nationalities were in the camp, all anxious to get home as quickly as possible and prepared to grab any opportunity to do so. Finding enough transport was a headache for officers given the job of sorting out destinations to so many countries. It was delaying repatriation, and the men were impatient.

A group of British soldiers, wandering around the airfield trying to cadge a ride home, came across an American pilot who asked them where home was.

'Wales', they told him.

'How lucky can you guys be?' the American said. 'That's where I'm heading. Hop aboard.'

When the plane landed, however, the Brits found themselves in New South Wales, further away from home than ever.

The health of the ex-prisoners who were still in Manila had improved to the point where, their craving for food now appeased, their thoughts turned to matters other than nutrition. A crowd of them visited a tawdry dance hall in the city, and it wasn't long before a big Aussie had a cooperative Filipino girl perched on his knee as he drank beer from a jug.

A local male resented this. 'We know Australians', he said. 'You no good, you surrender to the Japanese.'

It was like a red rag to a bull. The girl was dumped onto the floor and, almost before she landed, a big Aussie fist had splattered the Filipino's nose.

Some locals attacked the Australian, and his mates retaliated. In seconds, the place had erupted into a wild brawl involving dozens of men. They were going punch for punch when a Filipino produced an army revolver and started shooting.

The police arrived and, brandishing their own guns and large batons, waded into the melee and restored peace, but not before considerable damage had been inflicted on both the establishment and the faces of the combatants.

Fortunately, nobody was killed by the flying bullets. The worst injury was to a dance hall girl, who had a toe shot off.

Each day at the Manila camp, the repatriated prisoners were given a paper chit that entitled them to chocolate, biscuits, tobacco, cigarettes, cigars, soft drinks and three cans of beer from the American canteen.

The beer was very popular.

When word came through that the Australians' departure for home was imminent, plans were made for a fitting farewell party. However, three cans per man per day wouldn't be enough for a proper celebration.

Bodero solved the problem of building up a supply. He obtained paper and a typewriter from the Australian orderly room, telling them he had a lot of letters to write home. He copied the typing on the original chits, and the counterfeits proved to be reasonable facsimiles of the real thing. The only thing needed now was an officer's signature, so Bodero added an unrecognisable flourish. By signing them himself, he might be a counterfeiter, but at least he couldn't be accused of being a forger.

The fake chits were duly handed out, and the stream of Australians at the American canteen was now endless. The sudden drain on beer supplies must have made it obvious to the Americans that the Aussies were up to something, but if they were suspicious, they said nothing.

By nightfall, one tent alone held forty dozen cans of beer. The mountain of empty cans outside the Australian tents the next morning was proof that the final night in Manila had been a happy going-away party. However, it also meant that it was a sick and sorry lot who boarded the American Liberty ships that ferried them out to the British aircraft carrier *HMS Indomitable*. The carrier was anchored five miles out to sea because the harbour was littered with so many sunken vessels that a ship of its size couldn't get anywhere near the wharves.

The Liberty ships reached the *Indomitable* in rising seas, and the American captains circled the carrier, unsure about coming alongside.

Their caution upset the British commander of the aircraft carrier, who stood on the bridge, megaphone in hand, cursing the Americans for their lack of seamanship.

'Call yourselves sailors', he roared. 'If you can't bring those tubs of yours alongside, drop anchor and I'll bring my ship alongside yours.'

The embarrassed Americans declined his offer. Instead, they turned around and took the repatriates back to Manila.

The men, disappointed at the further delay to their repatriation, spent that night beerless in the same tents they had left that morning in the expectation that they would now be on their way back to Australia.

The British carrier's commander hadn't finished with the Americans. He came ashore and let them know in no uncertain terms what he thought of their seamanship, and then delivered an ultimatum: if they didn't have the repatriates aboard his ship the next day, he'd let the whole world know about it. He only had a few days to get to Australia, he said, and he was going to deliver the men there on time. If he wasn't able to do that because of their lousy seamanship, heads would roll.

The next day, the Liberty ships delivered the repatriates out to the *Indomitable* and although the seas were just as rough, they managed to get close enough for the men to judge the right moment to grab the rope ladder and clamber up.

It was a dicey transfer, but finally everyone was on board.

The *Indomitable* weighed anchor, and took off at high speed.

At long last, the men were on their way home to Australia.

CHAPTER FOURTEEN
HOMEWARD BOUND

THE Carrier's quarters were like a first-class hotel to men who'd almost forgotten there were such luxuries as bedsheets, comfortable bunks, hot showers, proper toilets and unlimited room to move about.

They didn't have fond recollections of ships. They remembered how the Japanese had packed them in like sardines in the torturous holds of the *Toyahashi Maru* and *Awa Maru*.

Compared with that, this was heaven.

The carrier's commander went to great lengths to make more space for them. He had the aircraft moved from the flight deck and set the area aside for recreation and exercise. Netting was erected around the deck so the men could play cricket. If getting home hadn't been so important to them, nobody would have cared how long the voyage took.

Despite the comforts, men were still dying. They had brought the thiamine-deficiency disease beriberi from the prisoner-of-war camps. Common in the East but unknown in Australia, beriberi was unfamiliar to the young medical personnel brought from Australia to care for the sick and suffering. They weren't aware that unless the build-up of fluids can be eliminated, the lungs fill and the patient suffocates, an experience similar to drowning. On the carrier, whenever the sufferers craved water, it was given to them. The water built up the fluid in their bodies and they eventually died, killed by kindness.

It was a tragic end for repatriates on their way home after suffering so much.

These deaths were in stark contrast to the way the victims of other tropical diseases were getting stronger and healthier every day through continued good food and relaxation.

Even men prone to seasickness were having a pleasant voyage. The *Indomitable* was sufficiently large for the heavy seas to produce little roll, and they were able to join in the amusement and entertainment. The carrier commander even arranged for films to be projected onto a large screen hanging from the ship's bridge on the flight deck.

The hours and days slipped by.

The sea and its fresh, clean breezes were so different from the foul air and dark interior of a Japanese coalmine, and the food and relaxation was a joy after so much starvation and slavery.

The men spent hours watching dolphins playing in the bow wave of the huge carrier, and picked up flying fish from the lower decks as the ship ploughed through their shoals.

Then came the excitement of seeing what they had dreamed about for three and a half years … Sydney Heads!

The repatriates, dressed in newly issued Australian service uniforms, crowded the flight deck as the carrier slowly made its way up the harbour. Then came the sight they had never expected to see again-Sydney Harbour Bridge.

'Hey, look', a man shouted. 'The coathanger's still there.'

Years before on the Death Railway the Japanese had tried to destroy Australian morale by saying that the Sydney Harbour Bridge had been bombed and was no more.

Jim Bodero, tears in his eyes at the familiar sight, remembered the Japanese guard who had boasted to him that Japanese forces had conquered most places in the Pacific and were attacking Australia.

'Takusan boom boom (plenty bombing)!', the Jap had said.

Bodero had rattled off the names of several Australian towns. 'They bombed, too?' he asked.

'Hai, takusan boom boom!' he was told.

'Burrenwadgee, that town bombed, too?' Jim made up the name.

Yes, that town had been bombed.

'The Sydney Harbour Bridge?'

'Hai. Bridge gone.'

'How many spans were destroyed?'

'Many, many spans.'

'And Phar Lap? Have the Japanese bombed Phar Lap?'

'Hai. Phar Lap bombed. All towns gone. Takusan boom boom!'

Bodero grinned at the memory. Here was the Sydney Harbour Bridge, without a mark on it. Phar Lap was safe in the museum, too.

The British aircraft carrier berthed at Woolloomooloo. As the repatriates filed off the ship, some kissed the Australian soil they'd given up hope of ever setting foot on again.

Buses were waiting to take them to Holdsworthy army camp. There, they were given brief medical checks and allowed their first sleep in Australia in what seemed a lifetime.

The next day, old mates who'd been through so much together were split up. They were being returned to the capital cities where they had enlisted-Fred Barnstable and George Beavis to Melbourne, and Chilla Goodchap, Ronnie Crick and Jim Bodero to Brisbane.

Everybody had lost track of Tellemalie, who hadn't been on the carrier.

'If it was anyone else I'd worry about him', Bodero said, 'but you can bet your boots Tellemalie will get back to Australia, even if he has to swim.'

And he did get back, although nobody knew how, and he wasn't saying.

It became part of post-war folklore that Tellemalie was in Brisbane working for the city council sweeping gutters. It was said that anyone looking for him only had to find a pub with a broom and shovel outside and they'd find him in the bar telling his tales to the drinkers.

Jim Bodero went searching for him and, sure enough, found him in a Fortitude Valley pub.

'It's bloody Bodero', Tellemalie said. 'Get sick of all that Nip tucker, did yer?'

'You're the only bloke I know who appreciated their menu, Tellemalie.'

'Have a beer.' Tellemalie held up two fingers to the barmaid. 'What are you doing with yourself, Jimbo?'

'I'm back in the newspaper game. I can see you got yourself a good job.'

'Temporary arrangement. I'm thinking of running for mayor.'

'How the hell did you get back here? You weren't with us on the carrier.'

'It's a long story. I'll tell you about it some day.'

And that was all Jim was to learn about Tellemalie's repatriation, as he moved on to discuss his home life.

'You wouldn't believe it, Jim. When I got back here, I found out that my sister was going to marry a Dutchman. A bloody *Dutchman*!' There was horror in his voice.

'You mightn't like the Dutch', Jim said, 'I mean, nobody did in the POW camps, but you didn't interfere in your sister's love life, did you?'

'Interfere?' Tellemalie gave one of his lopsided grins. 'Whenever he came to the house to visit my sister I'd get out my three-bladed pocket knife, strop it on my boot leather and tell him how many Dutch throats I'd cut with it in the POW camps. He stopped coming around after that.'

The years of imprisonment hadn't changed Tellemalie.

When the Queensland repatriates arrived at the South Brisbane railway station on 21 October 1945, they were bundled into fleets of taxis and driven through the city streets to a rousing welcome home. Bodero's brother had travelled from Rockhampton to meet him.

After the emotional greetings, the men were taken to an army depot and given another surprise: ration tickets. As prisoners of war, they'd become used to having little of anything, but they'd never expected that food and clothing would be in such short supply back home that it had to be rationed.

With preliminary procedures completed, leave was granted. Christmas 1945 would be spent at home.

Bodero had accumulated leave of one hundred and thirty-three days.

On 18 January 1946, he was discharged from the AIF after two thousand and thirty-nine days' active service, one thousand three hundred days of it spent as a prisoner of war.

The war left him with a painful legacy-amoebic dysentery, malaria, stomach ulcers, nervous dyspepsia, constant back, shoulder and neck aches and pains, arthritis, strained knee ligaments, continuous pins and needles in both feet, scarring to both eyes and malnutrition.

He wondered if it had all been worthwhile.

While he was slaving on the Burma Railway in 1942, a Japanese soldier had boasted to him that Australia would become part of the Japanese empire.

'Bullshit', Bodero told him. 'For that to happen, Japan has to win the war, and it's not going to do that.'

'We see, we see', nodded the Japanese soldier. 'Nippon win the war, but if not, no worry. Japan will own Australia, even if it takes a hundred years.'

CHAPTER FIFTEEN
THE PAIN

IT was a sunny Sunday afternoon in 1966. The war had been over for twenty-one years.

Steaks as thick as a Sydney phone book smoked and sizzled on the backyard barbecue as the sweating man in the apron sloshed beer on them from a bottle.

People who had been paying close attention to their thirst sniffed the air, put down their drinks and took up paper plates, holding them out like begging bowls as they edged towards the hotplate.

The cook, wielding his spatula with the casual dexterity of one skilled at his trade, turned the steaks over and moved them about like chess pieces. Blood and juices dribbled out as he scooped up a t-bone the size of an Olympic discus.

'Who wants it?' he called.

A fat man was first in with his plate. The cook flipped the steak onto it. 'What'll you have with it?'

'More steak.'

'Gawd, mate, you've got half a Hereford there already,' the cook growled. 'Give someone else a go. Who's next?'

The fat man waddled away. The steak filled his plate and drooped over the edges.

Even though his skinny body seemed to be crying out for nourishment, Jim Bodero hadn't joined the others milling around the barbecue. He saw the fat man's helping and felt sad. It would have fed his entire hut on the Burma Railway.

Jim closed his eyes. He was back in 1942. Around him on the hard bamboo sleeping platforms were fellow skeletons, prisoners of the Japanese. Many lay unmoving as death approached, others remained still because any movement shot stabs of pain through their wasted bodies. Ulcers had eaten into their limbs, beatings by sadistic guards had left broken bones and tropical diseases had ravaged their bodies.

The men wore loincloths of canvas or any other scraps of cloth they could find. Their nakedness emphasised the fleshless arms and legs, the bellies that had become empty indentations under xylophone-like ribs, the cheeks that were dark caves into which eyes had sunk.

They were all starving. The Japanese needed a railway built to provide a supply link between Burma and Siam, and the skeletons were the workforce, slaving in scorching heat from daylight into the night, fed a daily fistful of rice with an occasional stale Indian army biscuit and a morsel of rancid fish. The rice, dotted with weevils killed by the lime the Japanese added when they found that it was infested, turned a smelly yellow-green mess when it was cooked, but apart from a rat or two or the occasional bird, it was all there was to eat. And starving men couldn't be fussy.

Food was a fantasy for everyone, especially Peter Murphy.

Jim Bodero, his eyes closed, could see him lying there rubbing the sunken hollow beneath his protruding rib cage.

'Back home right now, I'd be getting stuck into a medium-rare an inch thick, with lashings of onions and creamy mashed spuds', Peter was saying. 'And I'd be washing it down with an ice-cold frothy.'

Peter ducked as someone threw the remnants of an army boot.

'Bloody hell, Pete, cut it out will ya?' the thrower wailed. 'I haven't tasted steak since Moses played full-back for Jerusalem.'

At that time, they'd been prisoners for nineteen months and beef was a distant memory, but now that Peter had started them all reminiscing about food, they couldn't stop. They talked of the pie, green with mould, they'd eaten after finding it in a deserted house when Singapore fell, the rissoles they'd made out of a bucket of yak blood, the rotten horsemeat crawling with maggots they'd scooped off before eating it.

Jim was brought back to the present by a plate thrust under his nose and a man's voice saying, 'Here, mate, have a go at this.'

A huge t-bone steak, sizzling in its juices, filled the plate.

Jim took the steak, but knew he couldn't eat it. Like every other prisoner, he'd dreamed of the sumptuous meals he'd have when he got back to Australia, but when he did finally get home, his stomach, shrunken by years of starvation, refused to accept much food. He ate like a sparrow, and remained skin and bones.

Jim looked at the steak on his plate. No man needed that much.

The wind blew a sheet of newspaper towards him that had been brought to light the barbecue and he picked it up. He couldn't get out of the habit of saving paper. Scraps of it had been valuable on the railway.

A headline caught his eye: *Japanese Buy Huge Queensland Beef Property*.

Another one! That's the third this year, Jim thought sadly. He could hear the Japanese guard telling him, 'Japan will own Australia, even if it takes a hundred years.'

Now, piece by piece, they were buying the land he and his mates had fought to save. It made a mockery of their wartime suffering.

Jim pushed the plate away, sick in the stomach.

He wished Peter Murphy was here. He'd have plenty to say about this.

However, Peter wasn't available for comment.

He lay in a shallow grave beside the Burma Railway, having starved to death.

POSTSCRIPT

BY CHILLA GOODCHAP, A POW MATE

Jim Bodero died in Lismore in northern New South Wales on 28 January 1991. He never regained his health or his weight after his release following years as a prisoner of war. When he died, he was still the walking skeleton he'd been when the atom bomb that was dropped on Nagasaki brought about his freedom.

I was a medical orderly attached to his work party in the coalmines of Japan, and had direct contact with him until the end of hostilities in 1945.

For about eleven months, he worked seven days a week as a coalminer at Sendryu on the island of Kyushu. Although his health deteriorated badly, the Japanese allowed no food rations for sick prisoners of war. To exist, he had to continue working to obtain the two small cups of rice that were issued to the prisoners daily.

Jim was injured in a mine collapse and suffered damage to his eye and body. As the medical staff had no supplies with which to treat patients, his frame and nervous system were badly affected, and he became a frail walking skeleton, but he was forced to continue working down the mine.

After the war, he returned to Rockhampton, where before enlistment he and a partner had operated one of Central Queensland's most prominent dairy farms. His health prevented him from continuing in this field.

Still painfully thin and suffering his agony in silence, he returned to his original trade of newspaper linotype operator. Later, he was to move to Lismore to ply his trade with the local newspaper. He lived in Lismore until his death.

Jim Bodero had never smoked when I first met him, but he took it up on the way to Japan in the Japanese hellship *Awa Maru*, the only ship in the convoy to reach its destination.

Crammed into the hold for six weeks while the ship weathered numerous torpedo attacks from American submarines, Jim turned to the smoking habit, as did I and many others. Who could blame us?

During two years as a POW working on the railway line in Burma, he suffered extensively from beriberi, malaria, dysentery, pelagra, tropical ulcers and skin diseases. Jim Bodero copped the lot. I was astounded that he lived for as long as he did. His will to live was amazing. Uncomplaining, he endured so much pain.

Repeated warnings to give up smoking had no effect. I think the habit gave him some solace from his ailments.

Jim Bodero's experiences as a prisoner of war transformed the athletic healthy frame of a sportsman and infantryman into a shadow of his former self, a thin, frail man who was destined to die regardless of his stubborn determination to live.

CHARLES A (Chilla) GOODCHAP, JP
Mermaid Waters, Gold Coast, Queensland